AUSTRALIAN RETROSPECTIVES

IMMIGRATION

JAMES JUPP

Series editor: David Walker

**SYDNEY
UNIVERSITY PRESS**

SYDNEY UNIVERSITY PRESS
in association with
OXFORD UNIVERSITY PRESS AUSTRALIA

© James Jupp 1991
First published 1991

National Library of Australia
Cataloguing-in-Publication data:

Jupp, James, 1932-
Immigration.

Bibliography.
Includes index.
ISBN 0 424 001667.
1. Immigrants - Australia - History. 2. Australia
Emigration and immigration - History. I. Title.
(Series: Australian retrospectives).

304.894

Designed by Steve Randles
Typeset by Solo Typesetting, South Australia
Printed by Brown Prior Anderson, Burwood, Victoria
Published by Sydney University Press in association
with Oxford University Press,
253 Normanby Road, South Melbourne, Australia

FOREWORD

Major changes in our views of the role of education and new demands for a freer flow of ideas between universities and the wider public make Australian Retrospectives a timely new venture. Books are by no means the only medium for the exchange of ideas, but they play a vital role in developing a tolerant, informed, liberal democracy. They are banned or burned by repressive regimes.

In this series we have invited authors to examine formative issues in our national history in a style accessible to non-specialists. A number of authors have responded enthusiastically to this project, welcoming the opportunity it provides to address a major question in a brisk and intelligently speculative manner. No book in this series is designed to be the last word on its subject.

As we enter the 1990s, almost every aspect of Australian society is under review. The ideological allegiances of the major parties have shifted dramatically. Politics is more fluid and the voters more volatile than at any time in our history. New causes, particularly concern about the environment, have become major elements in the political process. Our economic competitiveness and the future of our leading industries are matters of concern. There are fundamental changes in all areas of the media, including the development of new communication systems. The unification of Europe, the collapse of socialist regimes and the growing importance of the Asia-Pacific region have redrawn the world map. These and other changes will inevitably affect our view of the past.

By treating major themes over an extended period, Australian Retrospectives will bring a sense of historical perspective to bear on matters of vital concern to Australians in the 1990s.

James Jupp's study of immigration is an excellent starting point. Immigration has been at or near the centre of Australia's white history for almost two hundred years. It remains a vital concern today. The pace of Asian immigration and the environmental impacts of population increases are high on the current list of immigration-related public controversies. We are delighted to have this fine work of synthesis by an authority on immigration and multiculturalism as the first title in the series.

Religion, the nature of the Australia–US relationship, communication, shopping and consumer culture, right-wing politics, the history of policing, and popular culture are among the themes soon to be published or under consideration.

Australian Reprospectives is a timely publishing initiative. We have a talented pool of authors to draw from and a nation of readers demanding intellectual nourishment. We hope to honour their intelligent interest in Australia at a time when the nation is calling for new ideas and new ways of communicating them.

David Walker

CONTENTS

PREFACE

Few nations in the world have been so obviously shaped by immigration as Australia. Unknown to Europeans four hundred years ago, it is now settled by a predominantly urban people of largely European descent. Yet within that settlement process there have been important shifts, most remarkably in the past half-century. Modern Australia cannot be understood without constant reference to its history as an immigrant nation. Within that nation there have been different influences at different times, as the Tables reproduced here in the Appendices suggest. The sources of immigrants, their social, cultural and religious character, their impact on the broader society, have all changed over time. This short work helps to illuminate these influences, without claiming to be an exhaustive account. No such account would be possible without a complete survey of the past two centuries.

James Jupp
Australian National University
February 1991

CHAPTER ONE

BUILDING A NEW BRITANNIA

*M*odern Australia was founded as a group of British colonies between 1788 and 1836. In all colonies except South Australia and Western Australia the original purpose was to remove convicts from the United Kingdom and to use them to set up a new society.[1] Convict transportation had already been used in the British West Indies and some of the American colonies to provide a labour force: convicts were assigned to employers who had brought capital and equipment with them from Britain. Until 1834 slavery also existed in the British empire, but it was never introduced to Australia and British courts had decided in the late eighteenth century that a slave brought to England automatically became free. The Australian convict colonies were an extension of Britain in many senses: they were ruled by British administrators answerable to the Colonial Office in London; they were deemed to come under British law; those born within them became British subjects, including Aborigines. Access to the colonies was restricted very largely to British subjects, whether convict or free. Capital was invested from London and trade was directed largely towards Britain after the initial settlement had started to produce exportable goods.

Losing the American colonies by 1781, Britain looked elsewhere for areas to colonise, in the classical sense of settling them from its own population. The largest component of the empire, in India, never attracted significant numbers of British settlers and there was ample native labour for those enterprises founded by British capital. Australia, in contrast, was regarded as 'empty', as America and Canada had been in the previous century. Its native people did not engage in agriculture and commerce, nor did they settle in towns or villages, and they had no experience of employment or of a monetary economy. Early attitudes to Aborigines were not necessarily 'racist' in the modern sense; they were simply regarded as having no rights to land which they had not developed and improved. Their exile to the margins of society is best summarised in a letter home to England by a recent settler near Geelong, Victoria, in 1840: 'We have had a great many of the blacks about us today, more women and children: they are rather troublesome so I was obliged to drive them off with the stock whip on horseback. Nothing frightens them so much as a horse.'

In the first sixty years of British settlement, Australia developed from peripheral convict settlements to a series of distinct societies centred on growing towns, agriculture and mining. Such development was based on the expropriation from the Aborigines of their lands, the use of convict labour and the attraction of settlers and capital from Britain. While the society created from the convict system was often brutal, so was the society on which it was modelled. Britain had parliamentary government but was in no sense a democracy. Power at all levels rested in the hands of a small élite and the colonial social and political structure tried to reproduce this model. Exploitation of convicts, paupers and orphans was widespread in Britain and child labour was important in the creation of an industrial labour force. Flogging was a major disciplinary weapon in the army and navy and hanging was the penalty for a wide range of crimes against property and person. Exploitation and repression in Ireland, which contained 40% of the British population by the 1840s, reached its pinnacle with the famines of the late 1840s, in which one million died while food was being exported. The society being created in Australia was an extension of that in Britain and was therefore brutal, undemocratic and corrupt in its formative years. But by the 1830s there was a spirit of reform in Britain and an increasing search for respectability based often on evangelical Christianity. This influenced Australia, bringing the transportation system to an end in the eastern colonies, replacing convicts by free settlers and trying to recreate a stable and prosperous 'new Britannia' from very unpromising beginnings. This objective held out no future for the Aboriginal people, who were dispossessed over a wider area as settlement spread. But it was essential to the deliberate encouragement of permanent British settlement by mass, publicly assisted immigration.

The great majority of convicts sent to Australia between 1788 and 1868 were English, with the largest numbers coming from London and Lancashire. All counties, and within them most parishes, sent someone to Australia during these eighty years, but the majority came from the cities: crime was an urban phenomenon. So was political agitation in England, though not in Ireland. Much emphasis has been placed on such rural convicts as the Tolpuddle martyrs of 1834, transported from Dorset for forming an agricultural labourers' union, or the large numbers convicted of poaching under the English game laws. The fact remains that most English convicts were thieves from the big cities: most had previously been convicted and many were professional criminals or prostitutes, especially those from London. Urban backgrounds became even more dominant by the mid-nineteenth century. There was a strong representation from the industrial Midlands and the North amongst men sent to Western Australia at the end of the convict period. Many fell into crime because of the social conditions and economic uncertainties of the major cities. England was in a state of turmoil from 1788 until the early 1850s and even afterwards there were large slum populations who were brought up in conditions which led many naturally into crime. The rise in transportation in the 1830s and 1840s reflects the greater efficiency of the new police forces which followed the Metropolitan Police of 1829 (the 'Peelers') and replaced the inefficient parish constables. Transportation was seen as offering an escape from the gallows or from the overcrowded hulks and insanitary prisons. 'Model prisons' were built in England from the 1820s and Port Arthur (Tasmania) was copied from them. But the convict hulks on the Thames and in Portsmouth harbour were still in use throughout the convict period and English gaols were usually insanitary and overcrowded. Life at Botany Bay or in Van Diemen's Land was often better than the English alternative. The majority of convicts were neither flogged nor incarcerated and many eventually became farmers or property owners.

Altogether 160 000 convicts were transported between 1788 and 1868, of whom 111 000 were tried in England. London courts sent 25% and Lancashire courts another 12%, of whom some were Irish. Other major counties of trial included Yorkshire, Warwickshire, Surrey, Gloucestershire, Kent, Somerset, Staffordshire and Essex. These were mostly urban, industrial and mining counties, including Sheffield, Bristol, Liverpool, Birmingham, Manchester, Leeds, Stoke-on-Trent and the outskirts of London. These were all areas into which rural and Irish immigrants were arriving. Many convicts had been born outside the county of their trial. Of those on the First Fleet, nearly half were Londoners tried at 'the well known Old Bailey' or in suburban courts at Croydon, Southwark and Kingston. Right at the beginning Londoners made their mark in Australia. Other major trial centres were at Exeter, Maidstone, Bristol, Gloucester, Winchester, Salisbury and Dorchester, all in the south. The industrial areas were not strongly represented at this early stage, with smaller numbers sent from Manchester, Durham or Liverpool than from the county towns of rural England. But with over 360 on the First Fleet from London and its surroundings the influence of other English regions was almost submerged.

The great increase in convicts from industrial areas came after the Napoleonic Wars (1796–1815) and reflected years of political and social unrest in the Midlands and the North. Over four hundred southerners were transported after the 'Captain Swing' rebellion of 1830, often called the last English rising. This movement was directed against the use of threshing machines, which caused unemployment and was almost entirely confined to the rural counties of the South and Midlands. The largest number of machine breakers between 1830 and 1832 were in Wiltshire, Berkshire, Kent (where the revolt began), Hampshire and Norfolk. Only nineteen were hanged in the aftermath, but 149 were transported to New South Wales and 332 to Van Diemen's Land. Wiltshire, Hampshire, Berkshire, Buckinghamshire, Gloucestershire, Kent and Sussex were also the counties from which assisted immigrants started arriving in the 1830s and 1840s, some of them the wives of transported convicts.

A study of Gloucestershire convicts by Irene Wyatt of Gloucester shows that urban areas were generally overrepresented as the places of origin for those transported between

1788 and 1841 in what was still a predominantly rural county.[2] The seaport city of Bristol, the south Gloucestershire coalfield and the wool textile towns of the Cotswolds all sent more than their population might warrant, while the purely rural villages in which half the 1831 population of the county lived sent little more than a quarter of the total. What is known about other counties suggests the same pattern. In Sussex a large number were transported from Brighton, by far the largest town, though in no way industrialised. Among those sent from industrial areas were Luddite machine breakers transported from Nottingham in 1812 and a large group of Chartist potters and miners sent from north Staffordshire in 1841. It was often hard to distinguish those sent for 'political' offences, such as Chartism or trade unionism, from those convicted of breaches of public order. Many political mass movements in England up to the 1840s led to violence and even small insurrections. Industrial and metropolitan England were disorderly societies, quite different from the peaceful rural 'old England' increasingly pictured in popular literature and songs.

The majority of convicts transported from England came between 1825 and 1845, by which time urban convicts predominated. London remained the major source but the industrial cities were becoming increasingly important. Of those sent to Western Australia between 1850 and 1868 over 25% came from the North with large numbers tried at Liverpool, Manchester, Leeds and Newcastle. As with earlier convictions, there were also many from the metal trades area around Birmingham, including the city itself, Wolverhampton, Dudley and other parts of the 'Black Country'. Most of those transported were described as labourers (for men) or domestics (for women), but research by Peter Shergold and Stephen Nicholas suggests that there was a fair range of skills which were often employed by the colonial authorities.[3] A handful of convicts, such as the Gloucestershire architect, Francis Greenway, were from the professions (and were often forgers or embezzlers). They fitted well into the occupational structure and certainly more so than textile or metal workers, who would have found little use for their skills in the new colonies.

The importance of the convicts in stamping an 'English' mark on early Australia cannot be overlooked. Many were urban, literate, young and adaptable. The largest number came from around London and made a major impression on the accents and vocabulary of the English language. They tended to be irreligious and only a small minority had been involved in political activity, which even fewer tried to continue in Australia. In the peak years of transportation they made up almost half of the white populations of New South Wales, Tasmania and Western Australia. Once emancipated they became settlers or labourers and began moving into Victoria and Queensland. As the great majority were men, many of them lived a lonely and alcoholic old age and were falling upon charity right up into the 1870s. But some made a great success of their lives, became rich and, despite much prejudice, entered society and public life. Few returned to England and some brought out their families under the early assisted passage schemes. Their children and grandchildren were quite proud of their English origins but went to great lengths to obscure the 'convict stain'.

About four out of ten convict women were English, even though they were outnumbered by Irish women convicts. Most women had been convicted for 'other larceny' and gave their occupations as domestic servants. Within colonial society there was a distinction between 'respectable' women and those who had come out as convicts. Since the respectable élite included the wives of the governors, chaplains, and free settlers, the English were well represented. There was also an élite amongst the female convicts which included transported women who had become wealthy in their own right, such as Mary Reibey, as well as the wives of successful emancipists.

FREE MIGRANTS

England in the nineteenth century underwent enormous changes. Those coming to Australia as convict or assisted immigrants in the 1830s and 1840s were not from the same society as those coming in the 1880s. Many early immigrants could not read and write, as there was no national education system. The majority came from rural areas and small towns, although convicts were more likely to come from large cities and from industrial areas. By the 1880s the great majority of English immigrants were literate, as a public education system had been instituted in 1870. A larger proportion came from urban areas, although the immigration policies of Queensland in particular still sought and paid for agricultural workers.

The typical English immigrant in the first half of the century was an agricultural worker or domestic servant. More typical by the end of the century was a miner, a skilled artisan or a clerical worker. In the intervening years the gold-rush had brought out hundreds of thousands from England from all walks of life. The largest previous occupations on the Victorian goldfields of the 1850s were sailors or miners. Those who could afford to pay their own fares, who made up nearly two-thirds of gold-rush immigrants, often came from middle class or even more prosperous backgrounds, were well educated and politically aware. At every Census in every colony throughout the nineteenth century, those born in England were the largest immigrant group, usually outnumbering the Scots and the Irish combined. In the convict colonies of New South Wales and Tasmania the English presence was particularly marked. English immigrants were predominant in the founding of South Australia (1836) and Western Australia (1829). Only in Victoria, where Scots took a leading role, were the English challenged not as the numerical majority but as the socially and politically dominant element.

A number of myths about the English in Australia have been widely held since the nineteenth century: that they came to escape from the industrial revolution; that they settled mainly in the cities; that they were middle class rather than pioneering farmers and miners; that they were politically conservative; that they were more snobbish and deferential than 'Australians' (the majority of whom were, of course, of recent English origin themselves). Some of these myths reflect the contempt of the native for the immigrant; some were based on the reality of political and social domination from the English establishment; some are necessary to nationalist rewriting of Australian history which emphasises differences from the 'Old Country'. All are either quite untrue or must be seriously questioned. Many distinctively 'Australian' attitudes and forms of behavior can easily be traced to the English origins of the majority of early Australian convicts and colonists.

English immigrants were to be found everywhere—on the goldfields; in the coal-mines; on the farms and homesteads; in the industrial suburbs; in agriculture and business; in factories and offices. There were working-class strongholds of largely

English origin, such as Newcastle, and middle-class conservatives on the Sydney North Shore. There were rural English settlements in Tasmania and northern New South Wales and English suburbs such as Footscray (Vic.) or Hurstville (NSW). The great majority of overseas-originating place-names were from England. There were Englishmen in Government House and down the mines, among parliamentarians and paupers. Even the Catholic Church was originally staffed with English priests, although Irish domination followed quickly and logically after 1838. For nearly 200 years the Anglican Church (usually called the Church of England) was the largest religious denomination. Its nominal adherents were not outnumbered by Catholics until 1986.

To understand nineteenth century immigration from England it is not good enough to have a stereotyped picture of the 'pommy migrant' based either on myths or on later developments. The very term 'pommy' does not seem to have originated until towards the end of the century and was not widely used until the First World War. While anyone could be a 'new chum', the term was most widely used for the English because they were the most numerous. It is a friendly designation and suggests that eventually the 'chum' (a very English expression, also used in India and other parts of the British empire) would become like everyone else. Dislike of the English upper classes was shared by English immigrants, many of them escaping from rural pauperism and from a Poor Law administered by squire and parson. Democratic principles were widely held by those coming out in the heyday of Chartist reformism between the 1830s and the 1850s. While the cutting edge of Australian radicalism and lack of respect for 'betters' was often supplied by the Irish, Australia could not have acquired its nineteenth century reputation for radical reformism unless the English immigrants had also made a major contribution.

IMMIGRATION BEFORE 1851

Free English settlers began arriving soon after the first convict settlement, although their numbers were not important until the 1820s. Many were drawn from agricultural entrepreneurs, who often brought their labourers and stock with them, or from those retiring on a military or civil government pension, including some from India. Land was freely available, although some made their fortunes from supplying government or by contracting with government for services such as mail delivery. Entry into Australia was tightly controlled during the convict period. Permission had to be gained to settle, and land was allocated by the colonial government and so were contracts. This sustained a high level of patronage and nepotism, which was also characteristic of the government of England before reforms in the mid-century. Letters of introduction were normally carried by wealthy settlers, who had secured the support of a patron in England who would be heeded by the colonial government. These processes established a relationship between government and economic activity which became characteristic of Australia. Pioneers looked to government for support in the allocation of land, labour and transport and were not disappointed.

Gentleman settlers were significant in the development of Tasmania and the areas close to Sydney. In Western Australia a speculative element was more important, as there was no pre-existing white settlement into which settlers could fit. The Lancashire-born speculator, Thomas Peel, took a major if financially dubious role in 1829. In South Australia settlement was organised by evangelical Christians who sought to limit Catholics and to attract Anglican, Methodist and Congregationalist settlers from England. English settlement attempted to reproduce the hierarchy of rural England, with rich landowners, tenant farmers and labourers. Many of the early mansions in Tasmania and New South Wales, which are now cherished as part of the national estate, were created by these settlers in imitation of the stately homes of England. At least until the 1830s it was assumed that, as in rural England, the Church of England would be recognised by the State as the official religion. Some settlers, as at Kameruka in New South Wales, or Woolmers in Tasmania, created miniature English villages, complete with a church built and supported by the 'squire'.

This attempted reproduction of English village life was only successful in the early years of settlement. Many immigrants were not English but Scottish or Irish and did not accept the English model and especially its privileged role for the church. The evangelical and Nonconformist settlers of South Australia were not happy with the idea of an established religion either. While there was ample cheap labour in the convict colonies through the assignment system, this gave way under pressures from England by the 1830s. It then became more important to attract and retain free labourers, who were always in much shorter supply than in England and were able to demand higher wages and a greater degree of freedom than at home. In order to attract such labourers it was necessary to pay their fares. As the average agricultural labourer in the 1830s would have needed to work for about two years just to pay his own passage, this had either to be paid by his employer or by public authorities. Those wishing to leave their English villages could much more easily find employment in industrial England or go to North America. Moreover, most convicts and most individual immigrants were men, leading to a serious sex imbalance in the colonies and frustrating the object of building a permanent and prosperous society based on family life as an alternative to the convict system. Initially the assisted passages which began in 1831 were designed to send out single women, many of them from Ireland. But by the late 1830s there was a changed emphasis towards male labourers and their families. Thus began the various schemes of assisted passages, under which the majority of English immigrants arrived in Australia over the next 150 years.

Among those settling as pioneer landowners in the early years, a high proportion were English, usually from the southern and southwestern countries, and especially from Kent, Sussex, Somerset and Devon. They brought their workers with them from the same areas. Group settlement created some of the major early dynasties, such as the Archers (Hertfordshire) in Tasmania, the Hentys (Sussex) in Western Australia, Tasmania and Victoria or the Tooths (Kent) in New South Wales. Although John Macarthur was of Scottish parentage, he was from Plymouth and his wife, Elizabeth, was the daughter of a Devon farmer. At Camden they created a homestead and estate largely modelled on English originals. There was some settlement from the North, such as the Manifolds (Cheshire) in Victoria or the group of Yorkshire Methodists led by John Hardey who settled the York area of Western Australia after 1830. But the improvement of English agriculture which had begun in the mid-eighteenth century was most marked in the eastern and southern areas of England

and it was from there that many early English agricultural
settlers came, often bringing considerable capital with them.
When assisted passages were offered they were originally
most attractive to rural labourers from the South. Under the
English Poor Law Amendment Act of 1834, some Poor Law
authorities actually paid to get rid of paupers from their
parishes by sending them overseas at public expense. Of those
going to Australia by far the greatest numbers in the late
1830s came from Sussex, Kent, Oxfordshire, Buckinghamshire
and Bedfordshire. Early schemes of assistance extended help
only to agricultural labourers and domestic servants, the
latter being overwhelmingly their wives and daughters. Adver-
tising and recruitment took place mainly in rural areas, though
ultimately co-ordinated from London. A central feature of
the schemes funded through the Colonial Land and Emigration
Office was that fares should be paid from the sale of colonial
land, and that the proportions sent out (as between English,
Scottish and Irish) should be the same as in the home population; which meant that between 55% and 60% should be
English. This approach was adhered to until the colonial
governments took total control of recruitment by 1870. The
proportional principle was often used to limit the availability
of passages for the Irish, who were much more anxious to
emigrate than the English.

The deliberate object of reproducing the homeland populations was generally achieved, although the English were
usually slightly underrepresented and the Scots came in higher
proportions than the one-in-ten of the United Kingdom
which they have constituted for over a century. British-born
immigrants in 1861 were 55% from England, 28% from
Ireland, 15% from Scotland and less than 2% from Wales,
which was close to the United Kingdom proportions with the
drop in Irish population following the famines of the late
1840s. These proportions remained similar until 1901. But by
1947 the Irish-born made up only 8% of those from the
British Isles, compared with 71% from England, 19% from
Scotland and 2% from Wales, proportions which considerably
overrepresented the Scots who had been fleeing the depression
of mining and engineering since the early 1920s. By 1986 the
British Isles-born were 78% from England, 13% from Scotland, 6% from Ireland and over 2% from Wales. This again
was very close to the homeland proportions, with the Scots

making up for the historically consistent lack of interest by the Welsh. It was, therefore, not altogether surprising that 40% of Australians in 1986 declared themselves to be of English ancestry, twice the number who described themselves as 'Australian'.

Most of those brought out to Australia from England between the 1820s and the gold-rushes of the 1850s as free settlers, were from southern rural counties. Very few came from industrial districts, as migrants were pouring into these expanding areas, including many paupers and orphans from southern England and Ireland. There was very little Australian manufacturing industry into which urban immigrants could be fitted. The building trades attracted some, although England was also going through a building boom based on rapidly expanding population. Textile workers from Lancashire came out during the depression of the early 1840s, partly as the result of charitable collections. The colonies did not want urban workers especially when, like many of the convicts, they were from the city poor, without skills or potential. Miners were sought for South Australia from the 1840s and were recruited from Cornwall, Devon and Somerset. There was little demand for coal-miners before 1850 and it could not match the growing demand in England. Many unskilled labouring jobs continued to be done by convicts and former convicts, especially in Tasmania and New South Wales.

There was much disappointment with assisted immigrants. Paupers were rejected as unemployable, Irish servants were not popular and some of the women brought out from England were denounced as prostitutes. Many of the rural skills appropriate to England were of little use in Australia. Rural immigrants found themselves much freer than in England, where village life was dominated by farmers and land-owners. If they did not like their employer thay could move on. While Master and Servant Acts on the English model operated in the colonies, they could not be so effectively policed. As in England itself, those who did not like rural conditions could move to the growing capital cities. Employers and governments expecting deference and obedience found that many of the resentments suppressed in England could be freely expressed in Australia. Immigrants, though subject to periodic unemployment, also found that they could earn more, and eat a great deal more, than at home. Writing back to England they stressed these differences. To labourers brought up on an endless diet of bread and cheese, working in a wet climate, living in a tied cottage and subject to the squire and parson, Australia already looked attractive even before the gold-rushes.

The conscious goal of building a 'new Britannia' was followed in the sixty years after 1788 by government initiative in bringing out convicts and assisted settlers who were drawn overwhelmingly from the British Isles and in proportions similar to those at home. This meant that while the majority were English, the numbers from Ireland and Scotland were almost their equivalent. The political élite were largely English and Scottish, although many had an imperial background, frequently in India. But the settlement patterns, attitudes and behaviour brought out from Britain were not always typical of those left behind. The large convict element introduced an urbanised and footloose element which was much less important in England outside London and some major cities. The mixing of English, Irish and Scottish immigrants in the same settlement tended to erode the regional differences which were still so marked in the United Kingdom, especially as religious denominations were not effectively organised in many areas until the 1840s. A shortage of labour also eroded the hierarchical and deferential character of social relations still prevalent in the English countryside, where there was often a surplus of labourers completely dependent on farmers and landowners for employment. The thinly settled countryside, with its vast distances and its shifting population, was not a good basis for rebuilding 'old England' in the colonies. English political institutions were created, but they were drastically changed by the influx of thousands of liberal radicals during the gold-rushes. The English language remained dominant, apart from the German-speaking pockets formed in South Australia. But white Australians, although still mainly immigrants until the 1870s, were building a British society which was not simply a copy of the United Kingdom. Unlike their contemporaries in the United States, they were yet to build a society which was not British at all.

CHAPTER TWO

ENGLISH IMMIGRATION IN THE NINETEENTH CENTURY

The most rapid increase in population in nineteenth-century Australia took place between 1850 and 1860 and was caused by the discovery of gold in New South Wales and, more significantly, in Victoria. Between these years the recorded population of Australia nearly trebled, from 405 000 to 1 145 000. By 1860 Victoria had a much larger population than New South Wales and it kept this lead until 1895. From 77 000 in 1851 the population of Victoria soared to 539 000 only ten years later. Of this vast increase the largest number were English, 140 000 of whom were added in the decade, most of them straight from England but some from New South Wales, Tasmania and South Australia. The comparable rise in New South Wales was only 33 000 and by 1861 there were twice as many English in Victoria as in the original colony, making up more than 40% of the population. The majority of these raised their own fares and many were middle class or had been quite prosperous at home compared with the typical assisted immigrant. However, even at the height of the gold-rush, assistance schemes continued. Between 1850 and 1860 New South Wales assisted 39 858 English immigrants, Victoria 39 119 and South Australia 29 916. The English proportion was very high among the unassisted to Victoria. In 1851 two-thirds, in 1852 four-fifths and in 1853 three-quarters, of unassisted immigrants were English and came from social groups able at least to borrow a fare greater than a labourer's annual wage.

The origins of English gold-rush immigrants are not clear, as no effective records were kept for the unassisted. A large proportion of the assisted continued to come, as before, from rural counties — often with no mining tradition. There were large migrations to New South Wales from eastern England, particularly from Cambridgeshire, in 1853 and 1855. Somerset was important in 1852, 1854 and 1857. In several years Middlesex, including London, sent the largest numbers and it is generally true that Londoners were well represented both in Melbourne and on the goldfields. While there were a considerable number from Durham, Northumberland and Cumberland with a mining background, the Cornish were usually the largest contingent from mining areas, many of them coming over from South Australia to Victoria. Most of the miners were amateurs and little skill was needed to sink a short shaft. Farm labourers from Kent, Devon or Lincolnshire were just as able to do this as professional miners and were more likely to get assisted passages.

The population on the goldfields was very fluid, moving rapidly from place to place and living in temporary shelters and tents. The Victorian Census of 1857 gives a snapshot picture of where people lived in that year. In the mining areas the English (including the Cornish) made up 37.2% of the total population in Ballarat, 35.1% in Bendigo, 37.4% in Castlemaine and 37.8% in Avoca. They were less prominent at Beechworth, where one-quarter of the population was Chinese. In the major towns and suburbs they were even more strongly represented, making up 37.8% of the city of Melbourne, 47.8% of Collingwood, 47.3% of Richmond, 49.8% of Prahran and 40% of Geelong. In all of these they greatly outnumbered native Victorians, usually by more than two to one. Altogether, 36% of the goldfields population of Victoria was English in 1857. After the gold-rush was over the English seem to have been more ready to move to Melbourne than others, though many simply left Australia altogether. By 1891 over half (52.3%) of the English-born lived in Melbourne, as against 42% of all Victorians, 42% of the Irish and only one-quarter of the Chinese.

The gold-rush brought back a problem which had been at its worst during the convict period but had been slowly alleviated by assisted immigration and natural increase — the excess of males over females. By 1857 there were three times as many men as women on the Victorian goldfields. This imbalance had already alarmed English philanthropists in the 1840s, especially the Northamptonshire-born Catholic, Caroline

Chisholm. She began her work of resettling immigrants in the rural areas of New South Wales in 1840, paying special attention to the needs of female immigrants. She continued her work in England after 1846 and founded the Family Colonization Loan Society in 1849 which lent the passage money to intending immigrants. Her schemes supplemented and by-passed the official assistance programs, which had been responsible in her view for dumping immigrants in Australia without regard for their future. The gold-rushes greatly increased the viability of her loan program, and when she left for Australia in 1854 she had already sent out more than 3000 emigrants. Her main concern was that families should be settled on the land, and this continued to be a very influential idea once the gold-rushes were replaced by professional deep-shaft mining from the 1860s.

Caroline Chisholm's work, which combined voluntary effort with pressure on government in Australia and Britain, drew attention to the problems faced by women and girls when migrating to a country with a male preponderance. Women convicts had been exploited to the point where the transportation of women was discontinued altogether. Aboriginal women had been exploited by convict and free settlers, in the absence of British women. In the early years of the nineteenth century the exploitation and suppression of women was widely accepted when it only affected the poor. By mid-century, however, what became known as 'Victorian values' were becoming influential. The protected and dependent role of middle-class women was increasingly seen as desirable for all women. Family life was extolled by evangelical, dissenting and Catholic clergy. But, at the same time, there were few jobs open to women in colonial society, other than as domestic servants. The textile industry, which absorbed many women workers in northern England, was undeveloped. Work in the fields was common in England but was seen as unsuitable in Australian conditions which were dominated by pastoral herding. The wives of small farmers shared most male tasks but the ideal of family life limited their social role in communities where the main meeting point was the public house.

Women were thus consigned to a secondary role, as dependants of men to an even greater extent than in Britain or Ireland. Family emigration was based on the notion of a male household head, with dependent wife and children. Women were almost invariably classed as wives or domestics. Though their presence was essential to building settled colonies and their labour was essential to the family farm or the suburban home, the avenues open to them otherwise were limited unless coming from families with substantial incomes allowing independence. The trade union movement grew up on the basis of male leadership, as did the ex-service organisations which became so important after 1918. Politics was a male preserve, even while some Australian colonies were among the first societies in the world to give the vote to women. The immigration pattern, where men led and women followed, was very important in shaping gender relations in Australia for several generations.

IMMIGRATION TO THE END OF THE CENTURY

By 1875 England, Wales and Scotland were all substantially urban and industrial. Only Ireland was still rural, though with a greatly reduced population. The colonies still sought rural workers but were finding this more difficult. The idea that English townspeople made poor settlers was rampant as in the past. It continued to dominate conservative thinking on immigration until the end of the 1920s and, in extreme cases, right into the 1950s when the rural English had become a tiny minority. In 1877 a South Australian select committee considered complaints that recently renewed assisted passages were bringing out quite unsuitable urban English who were of no use to the rural economy of the colony. The committee rejected the emigration agent's proposed location of recruiting offices, 'in various large towns', and condemned 'the mistakes which have previously been made in bringing out so many unsuitable persons from the centres of population (which should rather be avoided) instead of the practical agricultural labourers who are most required'. Yet the problem remained that, as one witness told the committee 'the English agricultural labourer is very averse to move. They are very ignorant and superstitious'. While another witness favoured 'the villages and hamlets of the inland counties', it was noted that totally free passages were needed as 'not one in a hundred in an agricultural district could raise a one pound note'.[1] Caught between the eager but unwanted town migrants and the poor and ignorant villagers, South Australia abandoned assisted passages altogether from the mid-1880s until 1910.

South Australia was too poor to sustain much of an assisted immigration program, as were Western Australia and Tasmania. Victoria already had the largest population of any colony because of the gold-rush and gave no assistance for over thirty years. Most English immigrants towards the end of the nineteenth century therefore went to New South Wales and Queensland. The proportion of British immigrants who were also English steadily increased as Irish migration tailed off with the great decline of the Irish population. Cornish immigration was also reduced for rather similar reasons— one-third of the Cornish population left the country during the century.

Queensland, which only became a separate colony in 1859, was very anxious to fill its empty spaces and develop its agriculture by bringing in labour from any source. By the 1880s Cairns was a Chinese town and Mackay and Bundaberg were large Kanaka centres. Queensland also departed from previous colonial practice in giving assistance to non-British immigrants, mainly Germans and Scandinavians. Despite its cosmopolitan character, Queensland still saw itself as 'British'. Indeed Queensland became the centre of agitation for White Australia, as English immigrants began to pour into a society which was heavily dependent on cheap Asian and Pacific labour.

Like other colonies Queensland strongly favoured agricultural settlement and looked to the English villages for recruits. In this it was helped by the long-term agricultural depression which began in England by the late 1870s. The newly formed and initially successful English agricultural labourers' union supported emigration as a way of reducing surplus labour and improving the wages of those left behind. Despite the continuing conservatism of English villagers, these factors combined with the generosity of Queensland to increase migration from the eastern and southern rural counties, especially Norfolk, Lincolnshire, Somerset and Buckinghamshire. These were strongly unionised districts. In contrast to previous rural intakes, those coming to Queensland in the 1880s were mostly literate and aware of political and union issues. In 1884 British male, rural householders had finally been enfranchised in the last of the major electoral reforms of the nineteenth century. Those coming to Queensland included many of Liberal allegiance. While there was a strong Scottish and native Australian element in Queensland labour politics, the rapid rise of the new unions and labour party also owed much to this large intake of immigrants.

While many Queensland immigrants did settle on the land or become rural labourers, the English also made a major contribution to the growth of the coastal cities. By 1891 the English made up 23% of the people of Brisbane and of Townsville, and 21% of Rockhampton. The immigrant ships called down the coast before terminating at Brisbane and left a quota of their passengers in the growing towns. The English were particularly strong in outer suburban districts around Brisbane, such as Enoggera, Toowong, Moreton East and Oxley. By 1886 they outnumbered the Irish and Scottish combined in Queensland, a position they maintained into the twentieth century. But they were certainly not all urban. The majority in Queensland in 1891 were either farmers, labourers, farm servants, domestic servants or pastoral workers. The major counties represented were Norfolk, Lincolnshire and Somerset, which were agricultural, and Middlesex with London. Many came from the industrialised North and Midlands in the early 1880s and Queensland had brought in significant numbers from the coal districts of Durham, Lancashire and Staffordshire in the late 1870s.

The situation in New South Wales was rather different, as it was more urbanised than Queensland and had an important coal-mining industry. Many who went to Queensland later moved south, and Victoria often enjoyed English migration from its neighbours without having to spend any money on passages. New South Wales was often more favourable to Irish immigration than were South Australia or Queensland. New South Wales was attracting migrants from the industrial North and especially from the coalfields. The major English counties represented in this large intake in 1877–1887 were all urban and industrial—Middlesex, Yorkshire, Lancashire, Durham, Staffordshire, Warwickshire and Northumberland. This, indeed, marked an important turning point from rural to urban migration from England.

There was strong objection to the continued attraction of

industrial workers and miners, leading to a select committee on assisted immigration in 1880.[2] The colonial government had already ended its brief support for American immigration, against which the Working Men's Defence Association had petitioned in May 1879, arguing that 'on patriotic grounds, foreigners from France, Germany and the United States of America should not participate'. The main objection in 1880 was from the Newcastle miners' union, claiming that many who had described themselves as agricultural labourers had been recruited as miners. The combination of agricultural and mining work was quite common in England and this claim was probably true, though denied by G. F. Wise, the colony's immigration agent. In 1877 the most active New South Wales recruiting agents were often in mining areas, including Sheffield, Bishop Auckland, Wellington (Salop) and Guisborough (Yorkshire). Other immigrants were recruited from industrial towns such as Bradford, Manchester, Newcastle, Leeds and Bristol, all of them close to coalfields. In spite of apparent favouritism towards mining and industry, the official returns still showed that 55% of English male immigrants in 1879 were agricultural and general labourers. A suspiciously high number did come from mining counties however and an equally suspicious proportion were railed to Newcastle, the Hunter coalfield and Wollongong on arrival at Sydney.

By the 1880s the English immigrants were coming in large numbers from urban and industrial backgrounds, despite the intentions of the assisting colonies. Many were giving rural areas as their 'native places' but might well have moved into the cities like hundreds of thousands throughout England as industry grew and agriculture shrank. The tradition persisted that immigrants from rural England going to rural Australia were the most sought after, though it was often acknowledged that Scottish and German immigrants were even better. What Australian authorities worried about was the dumping of slum paupers from the larger cities. Perhaps this was a hangover from the convict experience, as there is little evidence that many such slum dwellers ever got to Australia at official expense. Indeed, as the century progressed there was a growing 'respectability' about Australia, just as there was a reduction of crime and vagrancy in England. Both countries were becoming more prosperous. The unsettled conditions of post-

Napoleonic England or convict Australia were disappearing. By the end of the century most English immigrants were thoroughly respectable family men and women, moving into suburbs like their thoroughly respectable Australian counterparts.

LABOURERS, MINERS, TRADESMEN AND DOMESTIC SERVANTS

Large numbers emigrated to Australia from particular villages in rural England throughout the middle years of the century. These included the thirty-six brought from West Tarring (Sussex) by the Hentys; 451 sent out as paupers in the 1830s and 1840s from the adjoining Sussex villages of Beckley, Northiam, Salehurst, Bodiam and Ewhurst; the forty-three from Tackley (Oxon) who were drowned in the *Cataraqui* off King Island in 1845; and the 186 sent from Thriplow and Foxton in Cambridgeshire in the 1850s. In Kent large numbers came from Rolvenden, Sandhurst, Benenden and Woodchurch. In Somerset the area around Ilchester sent many, recruited through an agent in the town. Even as late as 1873 many were recruited through the agricultural labourers' union in the neighbouring Buckinghamshire villages of Waddesdon, Long Grendon and Aston Clinton. The main forces behind this large-scale emigration from particular villages were either individual employers, active Poor Law unions, recruiting agents (as in south Cambridgeshire), or benevolent squires and parsons (as at Pytchley, Northants). Later in the century itinerant lecturers were employed who sometimes worked closely with officials of the labourers' union.

Such active recruitment was probably more important in creating a drive to emigrate than were economic conditions. Rural poverty was general but only certain areas seem to have sent large numbers through the assisted passage schemes. These areas include Sussex and Kent, Devon and Somerset, north Buckinghamshire, north Bedfordshire, south Cambridgeshire and north Oxfordshire. Later in the century there was substantial emigration from the eastern counties, particularly from Norfolk and Lincolnshire. Recruitment had to be based on personal contact and travel through the villages. Few read the local or national newspapers, which they could neither afford nor understand. In some areas farmers were anxious to get labourers off the poor rate (which they mainly paid for); in others they were afraid that emigration would reduce the availability of cheap labour. The task of the emigration lecturer was hard, especially if he did what was expected and went round the villages. Many preferred the town meeting and staying in a comfortable hotel. Among those who took on the job the most famous was Henry Parkes, who had himself emigrated from Warwickshire in 1839 and was to become premier of New South Wales.[3]

Most miners in Australia came from a mining background. Many were specifically recruited by mining companies with English and Australian connections. While the gold-rushes brought hundreds of thousands of amateur miners to Australia, those who stayed in the industry were normally from Cornish, Welsh or English mining backgrounds. As the coal industry expanded in the late nineteenth century they were joined by immigrants from the Scottish coalfields. Because they lacked a mining background there were few Irish employed.

English miners came from two traditions, which overlapped in some parts of the country. Metal miners, in lead, tin, copper and iron, generally lived in remote rural areas such as Cornwall, Somerset, Devon, Derbyshire, north Yorkshire or Cumberland. Their families had rural backgrounds and they frequently worked in agriculture when mining employment was slack or in the summer months. In the Pennine lead mines it was common to live in barracks miles away from the villages, only returning home for brief holidays. Such experiences were particularly appropriate to Australia, where mines were usually in remote areas and could not draw on a resident rural population because none existed. There were large numbers of miners coming to Australia from the 1840s to the 1860s from areas like Cumberland, Derbyshire, Somerset and Devon, but not from the Midlands. They were particularly attracted to the Victorian goldfields.

The other mining tradition, in which nineteenth-century Britain led the world, was in coal. The Australian coal industry in the nineteenth century was largely confined to Newcastle and the Hunter, Wollongong and Illawarra and (in Queensland) Ipswich. All of these recruited extensively from the English coalfields. It was the policy of the largest company, the Australian Agricultural Company, to choose miners from various areas in the hope (not fulfilled) that they would not combine as unionists because of regional differences. There were no coalfields which were exclusively staffed by the English as Scots and Welsh were always present, some Cornish were recruited and, less commonly, Irish as well. However, in most areas there was a predominance from three English counties: Durham, Northumberland and Staffordshire. These had certain traditions which became part of the culture of the Newcastle area. Unionism, consumer co-operatives, the Methodist religion, welfare and social clubs and labour parliamentary representation, were all brought to Australia by miners who sought to reproduce the conditions which they had developed in England. English miners (unlike the Welsh and the Scots) were reformist rather than radical after the unsettled years of the 1830s and 1840s. Many had acquired a reasonable standard of comfort by the 1880s, though this was always threatened by the uncertainty of the industry. They insisted, however, on controlling working conditions through the union and were led politically by men with a mining background rather than by middle-class liberals. Newcastle, Wollongong and Ipswich developed as Labor strongholds with many institutions and practices brought from England. In the Hunter this transference was even more complete, as many of the mining areas, such as Wallsend and Lambton, took their names from the Durham and Northumberland coalfield. As well as becoming a Labor stronghold, the Hunter also developed co-operative stores, Primitive Methodism (which started in Staffordshire) and soccer, none of them very important in other parts of New South Wales.[4]

Most of the early building and construction work in Australia was done by convicts. There is some dispute about how many were skilled and how many professional criminals or labourers. The quality of much stonework in Sydney and Hobart suggests that some skills were available. Convicts started the printing industry. There were many textile workers transported from the English industrial areas and shoemaking and clothing were two other industries well represented. However the ending of transportation and the growth of the cities between 1840 and 1860 made it essential that artisans should be brought out by employers and at public expense. Among those emigrating were the engineers aboard the *Francis Walker* who formed the first branch of what is now the Metal Workers' Union in 1852. Engineers were the aristocracy of English labour, being skilled and apprenticed. They travelled throughout the world and their union (then the Amalgamated Society of Engineers) had branches in Australia, the United States and Canada. While most major pieces of engineering such as mining pumps or railway locomotives were shipped direct from Cornwall, England or Scotland, they still needed maintaining. Foundry workers, too, began to increase in numbers during the gold-rushes of the 1850s. By 1888 there were several iron foundries in Melbourne owned and staffed by men from the English Black Country. In the same year several of the cement and masonry companies in Melbourne were owned by men from Portland, the major Dorset producer of limestone cement.

Because of the rapid increase in population in the mid-nineteenth century and the great wealth produced by gold, there was always a demand for building craftsmen. Stone masons were in great demand, as were carpenters. But they could only be attracted when trade was slack in England, which was also going through a long-term building boom. English trade unions, which were confined to skilled workers, kept their members informed about the state of trade and some financed emigration. With the spread of railways from the 1850s the English, who had first developed steam powered locomotives from the opening of the Stockton and Darlington railway in 1825, came out as drivers and mechanics. The increased use of steam power for shipping helped expand this trade, although in all engineering areas the Scots were just as prominent as the English and in marine engineering probably more so.

There were two problems in bringing out English skilled workers to Australia. It was not an industrial country and those already established resisted immigration through their unions and popular agitation. London printers had been unionised since the previous century and there were also strong unions among engineers, boilermakers, masons and carpenters. Quite substantial numbers were coming out in some of these trades in the 1840s and 1850s. They took an active role in establishing the Melbourne Trades Hall Council, for many years the strongest and richest in Australia.

MIDDLE-CLASS IMMIGRANTS

Most of those coming to Australia in the nineteenth century from England were from the rural and urban working classes, with assisted immigrants more likely to be from the countryside than were the convicts.

As a primary producing and pioneering society Australia did not seek many middle-class immigrants. Its legal profession was very small and many of its members Irish Protestants. Teachers were often brought out from England as were most of the Anglican, Methodist, Congregational and Baptist clergy. Middle-class women were recruited as governesses, but this occupation was very overcrowded and many found themselves little better than servants. Unassisted female immigrants were mostly middle class but few went into employment. In 1862 the Female Middle Class Emigration Society was founded by a Londoner, Maria Rye. This had some success in funding the emigration of governesses, some of whom were eventually able to marry into the families for which they worked. By the end of the century there was a wider range of middle-class occupations open to men and the shipping lists for the 1890s and early 1900s show a large number of clerical workers, many of them from London. Women did not enter clerical occupations in large numbers until the First World War. The two universities of Sydney and Melbourne were staffed largely from England, although academic numbers were very small. English-owned employers, such as the banks, import houses or insurance companies, also sent out English staff at their own expense.

THE NINETEENTH-CENTURY INHERITANCE

Australia was created in the nineteenth century. The major cities (other than Canberra and the Gold Coast) were established. The country was opened up even as far as the remote Kimberleys. The railway system was essentially in place although it took well into the twentieth century to connect up the Queensland coast and Western Australia. All this was accomplished by a small population in which the English formed the largest part. The English were never a minority. They basked in the glory of the British empire, even when they were very pleased not to be living at its heart. Throughout the nineteenth century the United Kingdom was becoming steadily more English. The Irish were in seemingly terminal decline after the famine of the 1840s. The Welsh were a small, remote though distinctive group. The Scots were accepted as equals although much fun was made of their alleged meanness and of their national dress. But the English were dominant: in numbers, in industrial might, in wealth, in politics, in religion, and in education. They were so visible as to be invisible.

It was not until near the end of the century that immigrants from England were obviously a declining part of the total population. By 1901 only 10.4% of Australians had been born in England, still a sizeable 380 000 but declining all the time to reach a low point of only 5% in 1947. Never again would the English be anything more than a minority, even if the biggest. As their Australian strength declined, so did the power and reach of the empire. But the myth lived on. Generations of Australians still looked to London as the centre of their world. Immigration policy still favoured the English above all others and they kept on settling in larger numbers than ever before, reaching a peak in 1981 from which there is only now a small decline. There are still more than twice as many English in Australia as there were at Federation—but there are four times as many Australians.

CHAPTER THREE

CELTIC AND EUROPEAN IMMIGRATION

THE CELTS

The nineteenth century saw massive population movements out of Europe. People emigrate when they perceive better opportunities elsewhere, when other countries are prepared to accept them and when the means are available for moving. All these conditions were present in Europe and, to a lesser degree, in those areas of Asia subject to European influence such as British India or southern China. Knowledge of the existence of other countries assumes some level of information and literacy. Most knowledge of countries of immigration was spread by letters and by newspapers in the nineteenth century, to people who were either literate or who had access to others who were. They had already been liberated to some extent from what Marx called the 'idiocy of rural life', which kept them at home in ignorance of the rest of the world. Events such as the Napoleonic Wars (1796–1815) uprooted many people, recruited them into large armies and navies and gave them an understanding of alternative styles of life. The spread of the British, French and Dutch empires also brought many into contact with other societies. Australia did not share in this vast movement of peoples until well after it had been directed towards North America. Distance from Europe and initial use as a convict colony kept Australia insulated for some years from movements which took many millions across the Atlantic from the semi-literate, if still very poor, societies of Europe and the British Isles.

The notion that immigrants are poor and desperate is

weakly founded in historical evidence. It may be true for refugees, but refugees in the modern sense were not a major element in world migration until 1918. Small numbers escaping religious persecution were important in founding South Australia in the 1830s as they had been two hundred years earlier in New England. Poverty and potato famines were important for Irish and Scandinavian emigration across the Atlantic. Such emigration was not a major factor in peopling Australia, though not altogether absent. Many of Australia's convict settlers were, of course, from poor and even desperate circumstances. Yet their level of literacy was above the English average. Emigration is usually evidence of the frustration of rising expectations, combined with a level of knowledge sufficient to be able to take some action. Most nineteenth-century emigrants to Australia, whatever their origins, were not paupers or completely illiterate. Many were quite well off in their homeland while others improved their situation very rapidly on arrival. They were, however, not highly skilled or well educated by modern standards. The majority of nineteenth-century migrants were officially described as 'labourers' if men and 'domestics' if women. The poorest immigrants were either directly recruited from paupers or were cleared off their land by Scottish and Irish landlords. Another route to Australia, especially for non-British immigrants, was to jump ship in an Australian port, although this was illegal under British maritime law. But it would be wrong to see Australia as a refuge for the poor and destitute once the convict period was ended.

The majority of immigrants were English. However Australians are not overwhelmingly of English descent and cannot be understood simply as displaced Englishmen and women. The only major area of which this is largely true is Tasmania. Elsewhere there was always a considerable Celtic presence from Scotland and Ireland, while in some areas there was an important German or Cornish input from the earliest days of settlement. Other national origins were rare until the gold-rushes of the 1850s. There were, however, at least eight Jews and nine Blacks on the First Fleet and individuals of Indian, Chinese, African, Greek or Italian birth can often be found recorded at the earliest stages of settlement. The first free settlers of Queensland were Germans, there was a Chinese majority among immigrants in the Northern Territory in the 1880s, there were whole villages of German Lutherans in South

Australia from the late 1830s and amongst the first settlers of Western Australia were West Indians and Indians.

By far the largest non-English component in early Australian settlement came from the Celtic areas of the British Isles. These areas included almost half the total United Kingdom population by the early nineteenth century. There was a population explosion in Ireland which raised its population to eight million just before the potato famines of the 1840s began to reduce it drastically to its present level of only half that. A smaller explosion took place in the Scottish Highlands and islands, followed by a comparable decline from the 1860s. Cornwall was among the first areas of Britain to become industrialised and among the first to suffer deindustrialisation as its tin and copper mines faced international competition. The only Celtic area which continued to expand throughout the nineteenth century was Wales, with its large coal and iron industries. It provided few immigrants to Australia in contrast to the other three regions.

The Celtic regions of Britain differed from England in several respects. Ireland was administered as a distinct entity even after its parliament was abolished in 1800. The predominance of the Catholic church made it culturally distinct and the Anglican Church of Ireland was disestablished in 1869. In Ulster, Presbyterians of Scottish origin were dominant and formed the core of the Loyal Orange movement which set up branches in Australia in opposition to the influence of the Irish Catholics. The persistent revolutionary history of Ireland, which led eventually to the independence of the present Irish Republic after 1921, made its politics quite distinct. Special laws were frequently passed by the London parliament which only had reference to Ireland, such as laws relating to land tenure and to public order. As the Irish Home Rule movement grew in the 1880s, Irish Australians were faced with a conflict of loyalties which many resolved by becoming Australian nationalists. Throughout the nineteenth century the English and Irish regarded each other as quite distinct 'races'. While the real differences were cultural, political and religious rather than physical, Irish were frequently presented in cartoons as looking quite distinctive and inferior. Celtic culture was described as incompatible with modern ideas, as was the Catholic religion. The peak of Irish migration to Australia was between the 1850s and the 1890s, after which it declined rapidly. The Irish took advantage of the assisted passages and nomination by relatives to a greater degree than the English. Emigration was common in Ireland as there was little industry to absorb the surplus rural population. But those coming to Australia were not necessarily the poorest. The real victims of the famines of the 1840s were those who stayed behind and died of starvation.

The quite turbulent and often disastrous history of the Irish in the nineteenth century was a major factor in their being regarded as a distinct ethnic identity in Australia. Their Catholic religion cut them off from the Australian majority, which included many Irish Protestants. After its initial establishment by English Benedictines, the church came increasingly under Irish control, some vestiges of which continued as recently as the 1960s. The terms 'Irish' and 'Catholic' became coterminous and rural areas of Irish concentration can still be traced by Census data on Catholicity. These include southern New South Wales, parts of the Victorian Western District and some areas of southern Queensland.

Irish immigration had some distinct features. As with Irish convicts, there was frequently a larger female component than was true for the English. The famines had left many families destitute and among the earliest assisted immigrants were some 4000 girls from Irish workhouses sent out in the 1840s. As one object of the assisted passage schemes was to correct the large male imbalance left by the convict system, Irish women were much sought after by recruiting authorities. One consequence was a high level of 'mixed' marriages between Catholic women and Protestant men in nineteenth-century Australia. The great bulk of Irish female migrants were unskilled and became domestics before marriage. The 'little Irish mother' immortalised by the second-generation priest and poet Monsignor Hartigan of Yass (John O'Brien), was a major influence in forming Australian attitudes towards the family and the role of women.[1]

Irish immigrants came to a large extent from the Munster counties of Cork, Tipperary, Limerick and Clare or from the central Ulster counties of Cavan, Fermanagh and Tyrone. Apart from those from Clare and rural Cork, this meant that the majority were English-speakers. The Irish language, spoken by two million in the 1840s but now by less than 50 000 as a mother tongue, died out rapidly in Australia. It was not encouraged by the Catholic church, nor was it the language of the majority of Irish immigrants. Most who spoke Irish could not read or write in the language, which had a limited literature. The only Irish translation of the Bible was a Protestant version unacceptable to Catholics. Thus the folk culture brought to Australia by the Irish found its expression mainly in songs in English rather than in the use of the Irish language or the preservation of classical Irish mythology. A large proportion of Australian folk songs, including 'The Wild Colonial Boy' and 'Moreton Bay' are of direct Irish origin. Unfortunately, the academic study of folk cultures and attitudes was not well developed while Irish migration was at its height and the undoubted influence of the Irish on the 'Australian way of life' remains at the speculative level. For most of the formative first century of Australia Irish Catholics formed at least one-quarter of Australians, with their greatest influence in New South Wales, Victoria and Queensland.

The major traceable Irish influences in Australia include the nature of the Catholic church, reformist and labour politics and public enthusiasm for some sports. Until the arrival of European Catholics in large numbers after 1947, the Australian Catholic Church was almost wholly Irish in orientation and inheritance. Among leaders of Irish birth were Cardinal Moran (from Carlow) and Archbishop Mannix (from Cork). By the end of the 1860s the bishops of Queensland, Maitland, Bathurst, Melbourne, Adelaide, Hobart, Goulburn and Armidale were all of Irish birth. The Catholic school system was staffed to an important extent by the Christian Brothers, an Irish-based order. Over the years the Irish-born influence declined, particularly in New South Wales. But Irish-descended priests simply took over the hierarchy. The last major Irish-born bishops were Mannix in Melbourne and Duhig in Brisbane. While the church and its schools both emphasised loyalty to Australia, the cultural development of the Australian people cannot be understood without acknowledging that at least one-in-five have come under the direct influence of institutions which drew their personnel and inspiration largely from Irish Catholics or from Irish Australians.

The political role of the Irish in Australia is complicated by the fact that many of the most politically active Irish in the nineteenth century were Protestants, particularly from the legal profession. Half the Irish-born elected politicians of colonial Australia were not Catholics and did not reflect that large part of the electorate who were. Nevertheless Catholic Irish played a greater role in Australian government than they did in Britain, where many were excluded from office as members of the Irish National Party. Victorian premiers such as Sir John O'Shannassy and Gavan Duffy, held office in mid-century at a time when Catholics were regarded with grave suspicion by most practising Protestants. But the greatest influence of Irish Catholics did not come until the second generation and between 1916 and 1956. Their instrument was the Australian Labor Party, which split in 1916 over the issue of conscription for overseas service. Opposition by Archbishop Mannix and the suppression of the Dublin Easter week rising combined to ensure that many Australian Catholics voted against the proposal.[2] While there were also socialist objectors within the Labor Party, a lasting effect of the party split was to elevate Irish Australian Catholics to leading positions in the party for the next forty years. This influence still continues in New South Wales. It was greatly reduced elsewhere by the splits in the party between 1955 and 1957 which gave rise to the Democratic Labor Party, whose activists were overwhelmingly Catholics of Irish descent. Among Irish-descended politicians achieving prominence between 1916 and 1956 were Ben Chifley, John Curtin, Joe Lyons, James Scullin, T. J. Ryan, Joe Cahill, Robert Cosgrove and Ned Hogan. There was considerable Irish Australian influence on the Labor machines in inner Sydney and Melbourne. Most of this influence has now waned. Irish influence in trade unions was less apparent than in Labor politics, but was marked in the building and transport unions. But despite the Irish character of the Democratic Labor Party and a failed attempt by Mannix to launch a Catholic party in Victoria after 1916, nothing like a strictly confessional Catholic party has ever emerged in Australia. While some critics thought of the ALP between 1916 and 1956 as an Irish Catholic party, it always contained elements from other backgrounds. When the split came in 1956 these were proved to be dominant. Since then Irish Catholics (now mostly three or four generations away from their immigrant origins) have diffused more widely throughout the political spectrum and have largely lost their firm identification with the ALP.

Apart from religion and politics, the Irish inheritance in Australia is often hard to identify. It is widely believed that Australian Rules, the most popular form of football outside New South Wales and Queensland, is of Irish origin. But this has recently been strongly denied by Professor Blainey in a well-researched study. Irish identification with the liquor trade and with horse racing has also been strong. Nineteenth-century Census data suggests that many hotels were owned by the Irish-born, though some were managed by Jews, who are not now conventionally regarded as involved in the trade at all. Irish Catholicism tended to be puritanical in some regards but this influence is hard to disentangle from the equally puritanical influences from Scottish Presbyterianism or English and Cornish Methodism. All settler societies in the nineteenth century, including the United States, were characterised by a struggle between liquor and gambling on the one hand and abstentionism and sabbatarianism on the other, which was also true to some extent for Ireland itself.

Scottish emigration was well established by 1788 and continues to be more pronounced than movements from elsewhere in the modern United Kingdom. Victoria was the most favoured colony, though there are pockets of Scottish influence in northern New South Wales, South Australia and Tasmania. Scottish migration to Queensland does not seem to have formed comparable rural enclaves while twentieth-century Scottish migration is almost entirely urban. The distinctiveness of the Scots rests on their Presbyterian religion, on their educational achievements and on a reputation for business and agricultural success. A substantial proportion of Australian graziers is of Scottish descent as are many leaders of the National Party and rural representatives of the Liberals. This underlines that many prosperous Scots emigrated and took up colonial land in the first half of the nineteenth century. While the majority of Scottish-descended Australians live in major cities, this reflects later migration trends. Scottish political influence, unlike that of the Irish, has tended towards the conservative parties although many of the founders of the Australian labour movement were Scottish miners and artisans.

Scottish emigration had several different motivations. Agriculturalists took their skills overseas because good land was scarce and expensive in Scotland. Highland Scots were forcibly cleared off their lands and encouraged to leave altogether by their landlords. Their plight was no less severe than that of the Irish. Urban and industrial Scots sought better opportunities for reasons similar to their English counterparts. Scots were particularly likely to be found amongst miners and engineers and in maritime occupations. Finally, as with Irish Protestants, there was an overproduction of Scottish professionals. Scots were more likely to be found as doctors than as lawyers, as Scots law was quite distinct from English. All Scots, except the Gaelic-speaking Highlanders, were better educated than their English or Irish counterparts, as official figures for assisted passage migrants consistently show.

The Scots served the United Kingdom in many military and administrative capacities and were prominent in British imperial commerce. They were less ambivalent about their loyalties than the Irish, who often saw the empire as a persecutor rather than a benefactor. There was little English prejudice against them and some respect for their education and success. Scots like Lachlan Macquarie occupied high administrative positions in Australia from the convict era onwards. Thus Scots were able to merge into the Australian establishment with considerable ease, especially in Victoria, where Scottish-born numbers peaked as early as 1861. One-quarter of overseas-born politicians in Victoria between 1859 and 1900 were of Scottish birth and in all colonial parliaments the proportion of Scots greatly exceeds that of Presbyterians in the electorate.[3]

The 'Scottish contribution' to Australia is easily measurable in terms of the commercial, professional, agricultural and political success of Scots and their descendants. It is less clear what the impact of Scots on popular culture and attitudes has been. While the Scots coming to Victoria in the 1860s were primarily rural and included many Gaelic-speakers, those coming to New South Wales in the 1920s were predominantly urban and industrial. There is no reason to suppose that they had common values or attitudes. The Gaelic-language culture lasted longer than that of the Irish-speakers, though most were also illiterate in that language. The Free Presbyterian chapels used the language and the Gaelic Bible. But this had all disappeared by the 1890s, leaving no trace. The large numbers of impoverished Highlanders who came to Victoria and New South Wales in the 1850s and 1860s had disappeared as a recognisable ethnic minority within their own lifetime, in contrast to those who went to Canada and formed Gaelic-speaking communities in Cape Breton Island, Nova Scotia. Scottish, Caledonian and Burns clubs continue to the present but many Presbyterians have merged into the Uniting Church and those continuing to identify with the Scottish religion are less than 4% of all Australians. This does not mean that Scottish-Australians have lost all sense of their original identity. Sir Robert Menzies, among others, continually stressed his Scottish origins and was admitted to the small Scottish Order of the Thistle.

The other important Celtic elements constituting the Australian people were the Cornish and the Welsh. In common, they were administratively and legally united with England, which was not true in important respects for the Irish and the Scots. They were overwhelmingly Nonconformist in religion, being mainly Wesleyan Methodists and Bible Christians from Cornwall and Baptists and Calvinistic Methodists from Wales. They were sabbatarian and outwardly puritanical. They were heavily concentrated in mining and many men who came to Australia became miners at some stage. But the resemblances end in two important respects. The Welsh continued to use their language while the Cornish had adopted English by 1788. The Welsh were reluctant to emigrate, while the Cornish were amongst the greatest emigrants of the nineteenth century. Cornish emigration to Australia was always associated with the expansion of mining. Cornish migrants came mainly from the southern end of Cornwall where copper and tin mining has been practised for many centuries. This was the area of Cornwall which had retained its distinctive language and culture the longest and in which Methodism was particularly strong. Thus many Cornish immigrants to Australia still had a sense of being different from the English. This was sustained by the concentration of Cornish miners in South Australia, in such towns as Moonta, Kapunda and Burra. They later spread to the Victorian goldfields in the 1850s and to the Western Australian fields in the 1890s. The Cornish were rarely found in coal mining, though some also went to Newcastle. They were particularly prominent in copper towns such as Cobar. Wherever they went, the Cornish were renowned for their mining prowess, their Methodist fervour, their organised games and their bands. The Cornish sense of difference did not extend to any close affinity with other Celtic people, although there were Welsh present in some areas settled by the Cornish and many of them were also Methodists. The Cornish had no particular grievances against the English and in towns like Bendigo they were markedly patriotic and enthusiastic for the British empire. Cornishmen like the Bonythons played an important role in business and conservative politics. But the Cornish political tradition was predominantly Liberal at home and in Australia. Because of the heavy concentration in mining this translated into unionism and Labor politics by the end of the nineteenth century. The South Australian Labor Party, the first to be established, had a strong Cornish component. This included the Labor premier between 1910 and 1912, John Verran, from the mining and Methodist Cornish village of Gwennap. The Hawke family was also important in South Australian unionism and politics and their descendants included the prime minister, Bob Hawke, and a premier of Western Australia, Bert Hawke.

Very little bound the Celtic immigrants together and religion kept them apart. Although Celts made up almost half the Australian population in the nineteenth century, they were always liable to assimilate towards the English. Perhaps half the Welsh, one-fifth of the Irish and one-tenth of the Scots could speak or understand a Celtic language in mid-nineteenth-century Australia. But there is very little evidence that any of these languages survived beyond the second generation. The Irish were divided between Catholics and Protestants and this rift became more acute as Irish nationalism developed from the 1870s. Scottish, Ulster, Welsh and Cornish Protestants were all actively hostile to Catholicism. Many were members of Masonic or Orange organisations from which Irish Catholics were specifically barred. The survival of national consciousness was expressed through Hibernian, Caledonian, Cambrian and Cornish societies rather than through Celtic organisations. There was considerable intermarriage between Protestant Celts but less between them and the Catholic Irish. Sir Robert Menzies, for example, had a Scottish father and a Cornish mother. Celtic Australians were subjected to the same patriotic appeals as those from England and many responded just as enthusiastically.

Education stressed the English inheritance and the history of England even in the Catholic schools.

To assess 'Celtic' influence upon Australia is, therefore, very difficult, despite the numerical importance of Celtic immigration. Distinctive Celtic communities disappeared except in areas in which they were heavily concentrated, like the Irish in southern New South Wales, the Scots in the Victorian Western District, the Cornish in the South Australian 'copper triangle' and the Welsh on the Hunter coalfield. Nevertheless Australia did not simply reproduce English culture and attitudes. The Anglican church was forced to compete with Methodism and Presbyterianism, while at least one-in-five Australians were Catholic. Liberalism was more popular than conservatism as a political creed and allegiance. Australians of Celtic (and particularly Scottish) descent were important in public and economic life and supported social and religious activity of a non-English character such as Presbyterianism or the Caledonian societies. Much Australian egalitarianism probably originates in the less hierarchical and deferential rural societies outside England. Australian nationalism, as it developed by the turn of the century, certainly had an anti-English tinge which was partly of Irish origin. The labour movement had a strong Scottish, Cornish and Welsh element in its origins and developed an even stronger Irish Catholic character after 1916.

OTHER EUROPEANS

The absorption of the large Celtic element into the majority English-language culture is readily explicable in terms of their common allegiance to the Crown and their common origins in the British Isles, where they had already been subject to English cultural domination in varying degrees. Other European immigrants did not have this background. The largest European component in the nineteenth century came from Germany. The British and German royal families were directly related and Germans were regarded as 'racial cousins' in the steadily developing ideology which came to justify White Australia by the 1880s.

German immigrants were very popular for their hard work and law abiding character. However, they were still aliens and this barred them from all assisted passage schemes organised

from Britain. Only in Queensland were Germans and Scandinavians actively recruited and assisted when the colony gained
control of its own immigration programs from the early
1870s. This preference for Germans ended abruptly in 1914
with the outbreak of war. All German immigration was
banned until 1925. The German-descended communities which
had grown in rural South Australia and Queensland were cut
off from their origins and gradually assimilated to the majority
English-language culture. However they retained their religious
allegiances and there are still substantial areas of rural South
Australia where Lutherans form the largest denomination.

The South Australian Germans were brought out through
a private arrangement by the entrepreneur George Fife Angas
and arrived in 1838 only two years after the colony was
founded. They thus have the longest continuous history of
any non-British settler minority in Australia and are an
interesting study in assimilation and in relationships with the
British majority. The immigrants came from Silesia in an area
which is now part of Poland. Some Poles and Slavic Wends
came with them and were a minor influence on South Australia. The Germans and Wends were fleeing from persecution
by the State of Prussia for their refusal to accept the official
version of the Lutheran religion. A common origin, religion
and dialect held them together long before Germany became a
single State in 1870. They were also geographically concentrated in villages which they had founded, such as Hahndorf,
Klemzig and Lobethal. They came to dominate the Barossa
Valley where the tourist industry still stresses the German
heritage today, though one more recognisable as Bavarian
than Silesian. The factors likely to slow assimilation were all
present and German rural settlers retained a distinctive life
and culture until 1914. They still keep their German names
and the Lutheran religion, though the German language has
almost disappeared. While other Germans came to South
Australia and many settled in Adelaide, the rural German
enclaves remained as almost the only example of a non-British
settlement created by immigrants. The Queensland settlements, in the Lockyer valley, retained their distinctive character less convincingly even though they were founded thirty
years later than the South Australian villages.

Punitive measures after 1914 reduced the influence of the
German language and the Lutheran church and cut the

Germans off from their homeland. German place-names were abolished, though some were restored in 1935. Germans were the only European minority to establish viable communities in colonial Australia and the wartime reaction was not only patriotic but assimilative. Germans had been successful in agriculture, business, the professions and politics. Many were interned and most were subject to discrimination. The Lutheran school system was ordered to teach only in English. It is hard to say how long the South Australian and Queensland Germans would have retained a distinct culture because they were faced with a deliberate attempt to eradicate what differences they had retained. The evidence suggests that religious adherence, however nominal, remains an important ethnic identifier long after dress, language, folkways and allegiances have withered. This has also been true for the Jewish population of Australia, which has maintained an organised existence for nearly 200 years.

An essential element in sustaining an ethnic community is the creation of families and the handing on of traditions. Most European immigrants in the nineteenth century were unable to do this effectively. They were single men who could only form families by marrying someone of another background, usually Anglo-Australian if Protestant or Irish Australian if Catholic. Family reunion with government assistance was only open to British citizens with the Queensland exception for Germans and Scandinavians. But most Scandinavians were single men, as were Italians, Maltese, Greeks, Poles and other Europeans, including the large number arriving in the gold rushes of the 1850s. An exception, and originally a minor one, were the Lebanese Christian immigrants of the 1890s who were able to set up a community which is now a century old and well into its fourth generation. But they too merged into the Catholic and English-speaking community quite rapidly and their descendants are unfamiliar with the Arabic language.

The dominant theme of nineteenth-century immigration was assimilation. This was inevitable for those who were unable to find marriage partners of the same background. It was also regarded as desirable for Celtic British citizens, both in Britain and Australia. Assimilation developed from being a fact to being an ideology. Groups such as the Germans and the Jews proclaimed their loyalty to the British empire. Many

South Australian and Queensland Germans became pillars of the conservative rural establishment. Only religious distinctiveness survived, particularly for Catholics, Lutherans and Jews. Today the origins of settlers in rural areas can still be traced by surnames and religious adherence, in the absence of more concrete evidence. In the metropolitan areas there are few remaining signs of suburban concentration traceable to nineteenth-century migration.

CHAPTER FOUR

NON-EUROPEANS AND WHITE AUSTRALIA

While the existence of Australia had been known to Europeans since the early seventeenth century and possibly to the Portuguese a century earlier, it had not proved very interesting to its Asian neighbours.[1] Chinese sailors were probably familiar with it, as important sea voyages of discovery were made by Chinese in the early fifteenth century. The same is possibly true for Arab explorers, whose influence reached as far as Indonesia and the Philippines. Polynesian sailors colonised the entire central Pacific without apparently making any attempt to settle in Australia. One explanation for this lack of interest lies in the very inhospitable north-western coast, which confronted most sailors from Asia or Europe. Another was the absence of any urban centres or trading networks. Indonesians from Macassar and elsewhere exploited the trepang beds of northern Australia, probably since before European discovery. They did not settle permanently but lived only seasonally amongst the Aborigines whose myths still describe them and whose language was influenced by them.

Asians were not important immigrants to Australia until the 1850s, nor did they form part of the world movement of peoples much before that date. Chinese and Japanese were forbidden to leave their countries by very strict laws. High caste Indians regarded leaving India to cross the sea as polluting. Arabs and Indonesians were interested in trading as were the Dutch, Portuguese and English after them. Maori settlement in New Zealand in the fourteenth century marked the greatest expansion of their extraordinary voyages. The closer peoples of Melanesia lacked the technology for long sea voyages. There was no particular motivation to settle Australia until Europeans provided both the motive and the method in the eighteenth century.

The only non-Europeans to settle Australia between 1788 and the early 1850s did so as part of the British settlement. Some were convicts, some sailors, some servants and some indentured labourers, all of them in the service of British masters and transported by British ships. Perhaps 3000 convicts were of non-British origin, including some from the West Indies of African descent. One of the first recorded in Australian history was Billy Blue, a Jamaican transported from England in 1796, who became a ferryman in Sydney. The transportation of servicemen and former slaves from British colonies increased the number of African and Asian origin by several hundred, though little is known about their subsequent fate. Early colonial Australians were not unfamiliar with non-Europeans but had more contact with Aborigines, who outnumbered them in the continent at least until the 1830s.

The first attempts to import Asian immigrants began with the ending of the convict system and the realisation that this might cause a labour shortage. A New South Wales Committee on Immigration recommended in 1837 'that the introduction of Indian labourers would be conducive to the general benefit of the colony', especially if it were to expand northwards 'where the heat of the climate might be too oppressive for the European labourer'.[2] While some Indians did come to Australia during the nineteenth century, the movement of labour was not comparable to that which took many thousands to the plantations of Sri Lanka, Mauritius, Trinidad, Malaya or Fiji. In 1847 the pastoral entrepreneur Benjamin Boyd imported labour from the New Hebrides and the first group of contract labourers from China were brought to Australia in the following year. These developments reflected trends in labour recruitment throughout the British empire and did not pass without unfavourable comment. In 1842 the Sydney politician W. C. Wentworth organised a petition against such labour, in line with his objection to convict transportation. At the very close of the convict period free labourers were already alert to the possibility that they might be undercut by contract Asian labour.

The continuing flow of British assisted immigrants and the lack of development in tropical Australia prevented a massive intake of Indian, Chinese or Pacific labourers in the 1840s. With the British 'opium wars' against China and the acquisition of Hong Kong, the Chinese prohibitions on emigration became ineffective and shipping companies began to transport large numbers of Chinese throughout Southeast Asia and as far as California. Chinese emigrants were almost exclusively male and aimed to accumulate enough wealth to support their families in China and eventually to return to them. The opening up of trade through Singapore and other ports of the European empires in Asia attracted more permanent settlers. In Australia the sole incentive to immigrate was provided by the discovery of gold in New South Wales and Victoria in 1851, an incentive which had presented itself already in California in 1849. The first Chinese gold-diggers arrived in Melbourne in January, 1853.

Immigration to Australia was not controlled in the 1850s and many of the Chinese had sailed from the British port of Hong Kong. Britain had no objection to this migration, from which its shipping companies often made a profit. The numbers of newcomers arriving in Melbourne was so great that any effective control would have been impossible, had it been intended. Yet, for the first time, the Chinese arrivals presented the threat that the half-million British inhabitants of Australia might be outnumbered, even though they doubled in numbers during the 1850s. Victoria passed legislation in 1855 to impose a landing tax on Chinese and set up Chinese protectorates on the goldfields to which Chinese were confined under an official protector appointed by the colonial government. This did not prevent Chinese landing in South Australia and walking to the mining areas. But a series of riots at Buckland River (Vic.) in 1857 and at Lambing Flat (Young, NSW) in 1860 and 1861 alerted the governments, now based on manhood suffrage, to the level of anti-Chinese feeling amongst gold-miners. This feeling was based on competition for claims, but also on the alleged immoral habits of the all-male Chinese diggers and on assertions of their cultural incompatibility with Europeans. While many officials defended the Chinese, the process of excluding them from Australia can be dated to the early 1860s and was based on popular demand and the response of democratically elected politicians.

Legislative restrictions on the Chinese were mainly repealed in the 1860s as the goldfields declined and they returned home or went elsewhere in Australia. The focus of attention moved to Queensland, which was just beginning major development in agriculture and mining. Despite massive assisted migration which reached its peak in the 1880s, Queensland was very short of labour and very thinly populated. Tropical agriculture was being developed throughout the British empire and Queensland seemed well suited to a similar development. As elsewhere the plantation owners imported labour under contract. For reasons of proximity their chosen source was the Melanesian islands of the Pacific and particularly the New Hebrides. A short boom in cotton caused by the impact of the American civil war (1861–65), led Robert Towns to bring the first group of labourers in 1863, starting a recruitment process which did not end until 1906 when the last labourers were returned to the Pacific islands under Commonwealth legislation. Cotton was replaced by sugar as the major crop and the peak of islander (or Kanaka) labour was in the 1880s, when large numbers of British immigrants were also arriving in Queensland. Altogether, over 62 000 were brought into Australia, of whom the great majority were men. Virtually all were illiterate but they developed a common tongue of Melanesian Pidgin, which is still used today in Vanuatu (New Hebrides) and the Solomon Islands. As with the Chinese on the goldfields, the Kanakas were regarded as unassimilable aliens and as competitors with newly arrived British immigrants. Chinese numbers also began to increase in north Queensland and there were riots on the remote Palmer goldfields in 1877. The immediate response was the passage of Queensland legislation restricting Chinese access to those goldfield areas which had already been worked over by Europeans.

The Queensland situation by the 1880s had several combustible elements. Large numbers of assisted British migrants were arriving and being allocated land or sent to rural jobs; large numbers of Pacific Islanders were being recruited for sugar plantations; large numbers of Chinese were moving towards the new goldfields; and the colony was thinly inhabited and had a fluid social structure. Racial tension was further heightened by continuing warfare against Aborigines, who resisted European and Asian movement into their traditional territories. The newly arriving immigrants in Queensland were also much more aware of political and trade union rights than were many earlier recruits to rural Australia. The peculiar combination of unionism, radicalism and racism in Queensland was produced by particular circumstances. At the same time racist ideology was becoming fashionable throughout the English-speaking world. Fear of Chinese expansion was widely expressed in terms of the coming 'race war' between Europeans and Asians.

Direct labour competition was perhaps less important in Queensland than in New South Wales, where the widespread use of Asian crews by British shipping companies was resisted by unionised seamen in 1878. In Victoria the main labour competition was in the furniture trade, where many Chinese companies had been established by those leaving the goldfields and settling in Melbourne. Union agitation eventually led in 1896 to Victorian legislation requiring that furniture made by non-European labour should be prominently stamped to that effect, a measure also adopted in New South Wales and Queensland, where the issue was less important. Many other non-European occupations were less attractive to Europeans, few of whom wanted to work on sugar plantations, as pearl divers or in tin mining. But competition in gold mining was so resented that Chinese participation was illegalised altogether by Western Australia when the Kimberleys gold-rush began in 1886. Chinese were widely employed in the pastoral industry as cooks and shearers, the latter an area of conflict with immigrant and locally-born labour which was becoming unionised. Chinese were also active as ringbarkers in clearing land for settlement and began to develop the banana trade in north Queensland. Other smaller Asian minorities were specialising in trades which often brought them into competition with the majority, such as transportation with the Afghan camel drivers and hawking with Lebanese and Indians. The increasing use of Japanese labour in pearl diving was also criticised, though few others wanted to join such a dangerous industry.

The position of trade unions and of the labour parties which they formed in the early 1890s, is readily understandable in terms of the long history of attempting to use immigrants to undercut local wages. But support for White Australia went beyond restrictions on immigration. Unions applied pressure to exclude non-Europeans from those trades where they had been succeeding, particularly the furniture trade. The Australian Workers' Union excluded non-Europeans from membership while insisting on union membership before

WHITE AUSTRALIA

employment could be gained in shearing, the sugar mills, mining and other industries which it organised. Liberal politicians extended the principle of tariff protection to cover the tropical industries in which non-Europeans were dominant, on condition that such workers were replaced by Europeans. Because of the reluctance of British migrants to work and live in the tropics, the vacancies were increasingly filled by Maltese and Italians, many of them eventually becoming cane farmers.

A series of colonial laws was already in place before federation in 1901. These either excluded Chinese from immigrating, or barred them from specified occupations or made it virually impossible for them to become citizens. At the same time general racial ideology justified the increasing control over Aborigines which included removing them to reserves, preventing them from becoming enfranchised citizens and limiting their civil rights to those of children or 'protected persons'. White Australia cannot be understood simply as a restrictive immigration policy. It was central to building a white British Australia from which all others would be excluded, whether recent Chinese immigrants or the original Aboriginal inhabitants. The *Immigration Restriction Act* of 1901, the first major Commonwealth piece of legislation which remained in force until 1958, was only part of the legislative armoury of White Australia. Colonial and state laws relating to immigration, occupations, citizenship and Aborigines must all be seen as part of a consistent campaign to prevent anyone from contributing to Australain nation-building who was not of European descent and appearance.

Immigration restriction followed on from a series of inter-colonial conferences in the 1880s and was a major factor in persuading the separate colonies to federate in 1900. These restrictions were in response to popular agitation, often organised by trade unions. The first national conference of trade unions, held in 1879, unanimously opposed Chinese immigration. In the following year the first conference of all the colonial governments agreed on the need to pass uniform laws. These were being resisted by some politicians, especially in Queensland and Tasmania, where Chinese were important in the new tin-mining industry. The arrival of several thousand Chinese into the Northern Terrritory to work on the railway influenced South Australia (which administered the Territory) into being the first colony to impose restrictions, followed during 1881 by New South Wales and Victoria.

Anti-Chinese agitation had become so marked by 1887 that the Chinese government sent an official commission of enquiry to Australia and tried to exert pressure on the British government. But as all colonies except Western Australia were fully self-governing within the British empire, these representations had little effect. Chinese passengers arriving by ship in Melbourne and Sydney in 1888 were refused permission to land, although many were legally entitled to do so. Two months later an intercolonial conference strengthened the previous call for uniform legislation and moved towards total prohibition as a goal. This led immediately to restrictive legislation in New South Wales, Victoria and South Australia.

The agitation for White Australia was fully developed by the mid-1880s and had moved from labour protection to openly racist arguments. This trend was sustained by growing popular journalism, particularly in the *Bulletin* (founded in 1880) and the *Boomerang* (founded in 1888). These were both aligned to the radical and labour side of politics and their development of a racist ideology through articles and cartoons had a lasting effect. White Australia moved from being concerned with the Chinese to being a crusade against all non-European immigrants. Queensland had already legislated to end the Kanaka labour trade in 1885, but political pressure from conservative politicians and the plantation owners frustrated this until after federation. The Commonwealth parliament passed the *Pacific Island Labourers Act* in 1901 under which the remaining islanders were to be returned to their homelands in 1906. The broadening of White Australia objectives, due largely to radical journalists, was well advanced as the colonial period drew to a close. Fear of the Chinese was replaced by a blanket opposition to all non-Europeans, and thus to the majority of the world's population. But as that majority mainly lived under European colonial governments, Australians did not have much difficulty in defending their position. China was regarded as weak and chaotic, especially as the Boxer rising coincided with the introduction of the restrictive Commonwealth laws of 1901. Japan was not yet a powerful State, though it became allied with Britain in 1902 and used this connection to protect its citizens overseas. Japanese were largely confined to the pearl diving industry in tropical Australia, in which they remained employed until 1939 under special terms of contract which did not permit them to become settlers.

The extension of prohibition from Chinese to all non-Europeans was endorsed by the intercolonial conference of 1896. In 1897 Western Australia copied Natal in British South Africa by introducing a 'dictation test' for immigrants. This was a device mainly used against Indians and Chinese in Natal and avoided the classification of immigrants by race rather than by nationality, as the British government preferred. The dictation test, which was incorporated in the Commonwealth Act of 1901, was discretionary and could thus be used for anyone. Western Australia was followed by New South Wales in 1898 and Tasmania in 1899. These laws formed the basis for Commonwealth legislation and marked a departure from previous colonial restrictions since the 1850s which had been directed specifically against Chinese. The dictation test required any intending immigrant to pass a written test, originally in 'any European language'. However, the language did not need to be one understood by the immigrant. The object of the test was entirely to facilitate exclusion rather than to ascertain whether immigrants were literate. A 1905 concession allowed testing in non-European languages but this was never implemented. The test could be applied to Europeans if there were reasons for excluding them. The most famous attempt to do so, in 1934, was a failure. The Czech writer, Egon Kisch, who was a noted linguist, was tested in Scottish Gaelic and failed. However a court ruled that this language was not within the terms of the Act. Kisch, who had jumped off a ship and entered Australia illegally, was able to continue his agitation against fascism which the Commonwealth government had wanted to prevent.

The dictation test was implemented until its abolition by the *Migration Act* of 1958. It became increasingly superfluous as shipping companies refused to take passengers who would not be allowed to land because of their non-European origins. The 1901 law thus established practices which lasted for over fifty years. These were extremely effective in achieving official aims without spelling out the White Australia Policy in

legislation which might have been offensive to Asian governments or embarrassing to the British. These practices included
establishing the right of Australia to exclude anyone from
permanent settlement, even British subjects; the operation of
a screening device which did not legally bind the Commonwealth to racial discrimination in law; the use of penalties
against shippers to encourage policing their choice of passengers; the creation of an international understanding that it
was not worth trying to immigrate if unacceptable; the possibility of deportation for those who had entered nevertheless;
the right to prevent entry to relatives of those already in
Australia; and the granting of a near absolute discretion to
immigration officers to admit or exclude on physical appearance or any other basis. While much of this administrative
structure is now common to modern States, Australia was
ahead of Britain, Canada or the United States in effectively
creating such barriers to entry. Some redress through the
courts remained but only in exceptional cases where individuals
had already established a permanent presence in Australia,
were British citizens or, like Egon Kisch, did not intend to
settle but only to visit.

The immediate victims of White Australia were those
already living in Australia. In 1903 the *Commonwealth
Naturalisation Act* prevented non-Europeans from acquiring
British citizenship in Australia. Those who already were
British citizens were exempt but the majority of Chinese had
come from China and were aliens. New Zealand Maoris were
exempt as British subjects but Pacific Islanders were not, as
the New Hebrides and the Solomon Islands from which they
mostly came were only British protectorates and not colonies
in law. These restrictions were not lifted until 1956 and 1957,
and then on terms which were much less favourable than for
Europeans.

Those who could not acquire citizenship had very limited
rights in Australia and could, under certain circumstances, be
deported. The Pacific Islanders in 1906 were often forcibly
removed to islands from which they had not come and where
they were not welcome. Some escaped deportation and their
descendants live in various Queensland towns, especially
Mackay. Apart from not having the vote, aliens in most states
were unable to own freehold property, especially agricultural

land. They were barred from public sector employment and were often denied hawking or other licences. They had no right to bring their relatives into Australia and many were faced with the alternative of deserting their families or returning to them in China. Chinese with British citizenship were active in defending the interests of their compatriots in the early years of the twentieth century. But the widespread public support for White Australia made it very difficult to challenge practices which most Australians supported.

All practices under White Australia were aimed at reducing and eventually eliminating non-Europeans from Australia, other than as temporary visitors. Exclusion of female relatives was obviously important in achieving this objective and was used as late as 1948 to keep out the Japanese wives of Australian servicemen. Consequently the non-European population of Australia (which was meticulously detailed in the Census) declined steadily after 1901. Chinese, Kanakas and most other non-Europeans had been overwhelmingly male and had no alternative but to remain single or to marry outside their community. Such marriages were not socially approved, but in contrast to South Africa and to many states in the southern United States, they were not illegal. The non-European communities which did survive are an interesting case study in cultural maintenance and resistance to assimilation in very difficult circumstances. A Chinese, Pacific Islander, Sikh and Muslim presence was maintained without significant immigration but in small and diminishing numbers. Those born in China declined from 37 000 in 1891 to 6404 in 1947. Those born in India rose from 5651 to 8160 over the same period but many of these were Europeans. Pacific Islanders almost disappeared, dropping from over 10 000 in 1891 to only 1637 in 1947. The Japanese were virtually eliminated by post-war deportation, numbering 3554 in 1901 and only 330 in 1947.

One community which escaped this decline were the Lebanese, who were Catholic or Orthodox Christians and of 'European appearance'. While agitation had been directed against Syrian hawkers in the 1890s, they were not normally excluded from settlement. They numbered 1500 in 1901 and had maintained their numbers at 1886 by 1947. But the balance of the sexes was better than for other groups and second and third generation Lebanese Australians were growing in numbers. The Lebanese case shows clearly that White Australia was based on physical appearance rather than geographical origin. Immigrants from Mauritius, Sri Lanka, India or the Pacific were sometimes of mixed descent but were accepted because they were not visibly different.

The White Australia Policy was almost completely effective between the 1890s and the 1960s as a form of immigrant exclusion, although it failed to eliminate all traces of non-European origins and culture, especially for the Chinese. In its Aboriginal dimension it was quite disastrous and the social effects are still being felt today. The ending of labour competition was not complete, if only because other acceptable immigrants came in to fill the places vacated by non-Europeans. Australian Chinese were largely confined to catering and storekeeping, though some passed into the professions from which they were not legally or socially excluded. Chinese influence in the banana trade declined and they were replaced to some extent by Indian Sikhs. An attempt to engage in shipping and commerce with China and Hong Kong collapsed in the 1920s, partly because Chinese-owned ships had been requisitioned during the 1914–1918 war.[3]

By 1947 there were still small Chinatowns in Sydney, Melbourne, Brisbane and Perth and many individual Chinese families in provincial areas running shops or cafes. Chinese clubs still existed although the Chinese media was almost extinct. Many Chinese had become Christians, married outside the Chinese community and brought their children up with only limited knowledge of Chinese language and culture. The community found it difficult to keep its links with China because of the civil war and the refusal of Australia to recognise the Beijing communist government until 1972. The revival of the Chinese community began with the arrival of southeast Asian students in the 1950s.

Other non-Europeans, like the Chinese, were limited in their economic roles to occupations which did not compete with unionised Australian workers. Indians and Lebanese were frequently itinerant hawkers or country shopkeepers. They were widely scattered in rural areas. The Queensland Pacific Islanders, who retained some of their original culture while being completely cut off from their islands of origin, lived a semi-rural labouring existence little better than that of Aborigines. While one or two mosques remained, the Afghan population of Australia faded away and camel driving was killed by the motor truck in the 1920s. The Sikh community of northern New South Wales was important in the banana industry and formed a small enclave at Woolgoolga. The main relic of the Japanese pearl divers is the cemeteries of Broome and Thursday Island. White Australia did not completely kill off the viable communities which had been created by 1900, but these were fading away or even disappearing altogether.

One unforseen consequence of White Australia was the settlement in north Queensland of large numbers of southern Europeans. As pressure grew against Kanaka labour in the 1880s, plantation owners began to look towards southern Europeans, in the expectation that they would acclimatise to the tropics more quickly than the British. Maltese labourers, with their own Catholic priest, arrived in Queensland in 1883 but the recruitment was a failure and major immigration from Malta to the canefields did not resume until 1923. Maltese workers were not welcomed by precisely those who had most vigorously supported White Australia, namely popular journalists and the Australian Workers' Union. But Maltese were undoubtedly European, Christian and British. They built up a strong community around Mackay, one of the major areas of Kanaka settlement in the previous century. The number born in Malta rose from 250 in 1911 to over 3000 in 1947, of whom one-quarter lived in Queensland.

The first major group of Italians arrived in north Queensland in 1891, sponsored by a local Italian businessman, Chiaffredo Fraire. Racial prejudice was evident in the Queensland government stipulation that the immigrants must come from north of Leghorn (Livorno). Union pressure ensured that they would not be indentured and could move to other occupations if they thought fit. Italian numbers increased in north Queensland after the repatriation of the Kanakas in 1906 until by 1933 there were more in Queensland than in any other state. The main Italian settlements were Ingham, Tully and Innisfail, all sugar growing areas. Other European immigrants, including Finns, Croatians and Greeks also worked on the canefields, many filling jobs previously undertaken by Kanakas. This led to a Queensland government enquiry in 1925 into alien labour (the Ferry Report) and to the introduction of British quotas by the Australian Workers' Union in

1930 as the depression reduced employment. In Queensland, as previously, the twin objectives of protecting labour conditions and preserving racial purity were still very important in the 1920s but were now directed against southern Europeans.

Much debate about the White Australia Policy has tried to disentangle the objective of preserving labour conditions from that of maintaining racial purity. This can be a frustrating exercise. The policy statements of the labour and trade union movements between the 1870s and the 1950s did not make this distinction. The first national platform of the Australian Labor Party called for the development of an Australian national sentiment based on the maintenance of racial purity. Those who regard the search for an Australian national identity as desirable are often totally opposed to racism. Yet that was not the case in 1906. Equally, those who support the aims of the labour and socialist movement are normally internationalists believing in the brotherhood of man (or the sisterhood of women). That was not a central belief of the nineteenth-century labour movement, except as an oratorical device. It is a misreading of history to argue that White Australia was 'really' about preventing wages from being undercut. It was quite simply what it appears to be from the considerable volume of contemporary writing and speech-making—an assertion that the white race was superior to all others and must preserve that superiority by excluding all others from the continent. White Australia was an ideology, not just a method of controlling immigration. It appealed to a wide variety of Australians, including the large numbers of British working-class immigrants who were pouring in between 1880 and 1930 when the policy was being most rigorously upheld.

CHAPTER FIVE

BRITISH IMMIGRATION IN THE TWENTIETH CENTURY

*I*n the nineteenth century Britain stood at the centre of the greatest empire in world history, on which 'the sun never set' from Fiji to western Canada. When Queen Victoria celebrated her diamond jubilee in 1897 there was no public recognition that this state of affairs would ever change. The Boer War of 1899–1902 was greeted with wild patriotism both in England and Australia. It was the beginning of the end. Ireland revolted in 1916 and by 1921 most of it was effectively independent. The two world wars of 1914–1918 and 1939–1945 greatly weakened Britain, putting it in debt and straining its domestic economy. British development was contradictory: rich and powerful, the workshop of the world and the centre of the universe (as Piccadilly Circus, London, was widely called); yet also leaving millions in rural poverty and urban squalor and with its Irish backyard famine-struck and decimated by emigration. The English aristocracy and plutocracy was at its height in the years before 1914. Industrial workers in the Midlands and clerical workers in London were mostly living in solid brick houses with running water and gas, though frequently without bathrooms. Yet the slums of east London, Liverpool, Glasgow, Manchester or Leeds were world famous. Christian missionaries went in search of 'darkest England', which they could easily find within a mile or two of Parliament and Buckingham Palace.

British living standards rose throughout the nineteenth century, as did the quality of housing, public health and education. Public transport allowed workers to live away from their workplaces, starting the massive suburbanisation which characterised both England and Australia by 1900. The introduction of old age pensions in 1908 reduced the shadow of the workhouse over the rural poor, although they remained open until 1948. The sweated trades and outwork were denounced and legislated against in the 1890s, at the same time as they were causing concern in Melbourne. Child labour was greatly reduced by the free and compulsory education system to the age of twelve, which was in place by 1899. Women still made up the majority of cotton textile workers, harvested in the fields and went into domestic service right up to 1939. But the idea was growing that respectable families did not send their wives out to work. On the coalfields there was little alternative employment for women in any case. When the depression hit Britain in the late 1920s it was worst in areas dominated by male employment such as mining and heavy engineering. This model of respectability was very influential in Australia, which also found whole families made destitute after 1929, because the male breadwinner was out of work and there was little employment for their wives.

As British living standards rose so did expectations. Emigration often marked disatisfaction with living standards that were getting better too slowly, rather than utter desperation at conditions of abject poverty. There is little evidence that the really poor and destitute ever got to Australia in large numbers from England after the second half of the nineteenth century. Emigration recruiters were warned against sending paupers and far more went to Canada than to Australia. Charities in the London East End and the unemployment assistance authorities sent out several thousand Londoners between the 1880s and 1914, mostly from the unskilled trades such as waterside workers, van boys or carters. There was no objection to anyone coming from England who could raise the fare but Australian colonies did not seek out the unskilled urban worker. They still wanted rural labourers and advertised extensively for agricultural and domestic workers right through the 1920s. The typical immigrant was from the more ambitious working class, especially from London and southeast England. As the English economy became depressed in the 1920s many miners and industrial workers from Scotland, the North and the Midlands were also attracted. But Australian industry was poorly developed, There was no assured employment for cotton workers, for skilled engineers, for shipbuilders or for many other trades which had become specialised and organised by craft unions. When the depression struck in 1929 there was much distress amongst recently arrived immigrants, many of whom had left home to escape unemployment.

The major factors prompting emigration from Britain between 1900 and 1930 were: the continuing recruitment and assistance campaigns by the states and, after 1920, by the Commonwealth; the decline of major industries, especially coal mining; rising expectations which were not being met; industrial unrest; and post-war restlessness. The most severely depressed areas were in the Celtic fringe; south Wales, Scotland, Northern Ireland and Cornwall. English areas were also affected, including Durham and Northumberland, Cumberland and Lancashire. The largest source of English immigrants continued to be London and the Southeast, which had relatively high levels of employment and were expanding throughout the inter-war years. The long-term unemployed were in rather the same position as the nineteenth-century paupers — they could not afford to emigrate and they were not sought after by Australia. These conditions were at their most acute while Australia was also depressed, in the early 1930s. There was almost no immigration in these years and many returned home, where social service provision was better.

The memory of these years was still strong when the post-war program began in 1946. Australia had abandoned its search for rural and domestic workers from Britain, as few were available. Domestic service almost disappeared during the war. Agriculture was greatly expanded by the need to produce food in England to escape German submarine attacks and, later, to conserve foreign exchange. Agricultural labourers continued to leave the land, but mainly to work in urban jobs of which there was no shortage in the 1950s and 1960s. Under the slogan 'populate or perish' Australia was willing to accept most occupations although at first preference was given to skilled tradesmen, especially in building and construction. London remained the major source of emigrants as it also had the worst housing shortage, caused by wartime bombing, inter-war migration and post-war slum clearance.

Australian migration offices in Manchester, and in the late 1960s in Leeds and Birmingham, were able to recruit many thousands and the Northwest (Manchester and Liverpool) has usually been the second major source of migrants after

"Populate or Perish"

London and the Southeast. At the same time as hundreds of thousands were leaving the London area for Australia and Canada, similar numbers were coming in from the West Indies, India and Ireland. There was a steady population drift towards the South and out of London to surrounding towns such as Crawley, Stevenage, Luton, Southend and Cambridge. In the thirty years from 1951 greater London lost 2 000 000 people.

Emigration to Australia was thus part of a general shifting of population which was most marked in the London region and the Northwest. Rural counties sent few migrants and neither did the coalfields. Skilled workers were attracted from the steel and shipbuilding industries by BHP (Broken Hill Proprietary Limited) and into the rapidly growing metal trades and motor manufacturing. By the 1970s Australia had a well-developed and diversified industrial structure, which urban workers could fit into much more easily than had been true before 1930.

Britain was increasingly prosperous throughout the 1950s and 1960s but this did not inhibit emigration to Australia. British housing was being rapidly improved, with the provision of bathrooms rising from about 50% in 1945 to over 95% by 1985. Legislation encouraged the improvement of the large stock of old housing while public housing catered for 30% of the population. Home purchase became common and by the 1980s a majority were buying or already owned the house in which they lived. Eventually the economic differential between England and Australia was reduced to the level where the incentive to emigrate was quite marginal. When another depression came by 1980 there was no surge to Australia. Too many people had invested in their own homes to move; too many were still in well-paid jobs in the south; too many enjoyed working conditions, holidays and leisure beyond the dreams of their parents. In 1982 assisted passages were ended by the Australian Liberal government. After 150 years the British were no longer privileged. If they wanted to come to Australia they had to pay their own fares or find an employer ready to do so. The industries declining in Britain were also in trouble in Australia. Both societies were now turning to services, white collar and professional employment. British emigrants were frequently middle class from the suburbs of large cities—coming to Australia to be middle class in the suburbs of big cities.

ASSISTED PASSAGES

A WORKING-CLASS MIGRATION:
1900–1929

The depression of the 1890s ended immigration for the next fifteen years, except for Western Australia where the last of the gold-rushes began in 1892. Most migration to Western Australia was from other colonies but its English-born population rose from 9634 to 33 278 between 1891 and 1911. Everywhere else recorded a continuing decline in the English population over the same period. With an economic recovery, assisted immigration began again in 1907, continued until the outbreak of war in 1914 and resumed in 1920, after which the Commonwealth took over full control from the states. This boom in immigration ended in 1929 with the onset of the world depression. For the next few years more people returned to England than came out. Despite a brief revival in 1938, the intervention of the war of 1939–1945 meant that there was no net English immigration between 1929 and 1947. The English became a small minority, although still by far the largest immigrant group, in a population which was overwhelmingly Australian-born and which was often nationalistic and increasingly 'anti-pommy'.

Between 1901 and 1933 the English-born population of Australia rose from 393 321 (including Wales) to 486 831. The peak years for arrivals had been 1910–1913 and 1923–1927. Although official policy still stressed the need for agricultural settlers, this aim was becoming increasingly unrealistic. England and Scotland were overwhelmingly urban and rural Ireland almost ceased sending immigrants after independence was gained in 1921. Moreover, the settlement prospects in rural Australia were not very good outside Queensland. Disastrous attempts to settle returned soldiers in Western Australia and Victoria collapsed by the end of the 1920s, leading to official enquiries which found that 'closer settlement' was economically not viable. Various schemes to put orphans and juniors on the land continued, such as the Big Brother Movement (founded in 1925 and still existing) and the Fairbridge Farm scheme. Some of these immigrants remained successful in agriculture, but most went to the cities, especially during the depression of the 1930s. Rural immigration had become a 'myth', very attractive to the newly created Country Party and to conservatives who still thought in terms of rural values and the 'yeoman farmer', but disastrous for many of those from England who were tempted by official propaganda.

While the states controlled immigration they continued to seek the same kind of immigrants as had come out in the nineteenth century. The *Oswestry Grange*, bound from London for Queensland ports in August 1910, carried sixty-six English domestic servants, fifteeen agricultural labourers, fifteen skilled urban workers, eleven unskilled urban workers and one salesman. Many of the urban workers were from the railways. There were no professional or white collar assisted-immigrant passengers. Queensland was still developing and passenger lists to the southern Australian ports already had a higher urban working class component. Fifty-seven of the English passengers on the *Orontes* which left London in September 1910, for Fremantle, Adelaide, Melbourne and Sydney, were unskilled urban workers, mostly described as labourers; forty-four were skilled workers, nearly all engineers and mechanics; only ten were in agriculture, five in domestic service and one a miner. The *Norseman*, sailing for Melbourne, Sydney and Brisbane in June 1910, carried eighty-one unskilled English workers, seventy-six agricultural workers, twenty-nine skilled workers, twenty domestics, seventeen clerical and sales persons, six miners and one professional. The big exception to this pattern of bringing out urban workers was Western Australia, which still sought primary industry workers. The *Armadale*, which left London for Fremantle in November 1910, took 264 agricultural workers, forty-two domestic servants and only one skilled worker. The *Rimutaka*, sailing for Albany later in the same month, took 100 agriculturalists and gardeners, seventy-eight domestic servants, seventy unskilled workers, three white collar workers and one skilled worker. The English going to Western Australia were drawn from very similar backgrounds to the nineteenth-century migrants — agricultural labourers and domestic servants.[1]

The English migration prior to 1914 had several characteristics. The English now made up the great majority of those coming from Britain. Most were unskilled and the three largest occupations were usually labourers, agricultural workers and domestic servants. Most were fairly badly educated although literate. They were essentially working class, though not from such highly organised and unionised occupations as miners, textile workers or engineers. Very few women had any occupation other than domestic servant. Most of the English were family men in their twenties and thirties, with their wives and children (often in quite large numbers). Few had any developed skills and the women were all cast in a domestic mould. The traditional Australian emphasis on hard manual work, on home creation and the virtues of the common man, were thoroughly engrained in those coming out from England before the First World War. Many of the men were to find a useful role in the AIF (Australian Imperial Force), of whom nearly one-in-five were English-born.

Between 1907 and 1914, 182 000 assisted immigrants arrived in Australia, of whom about 80% were English. They went mainly to Queensland, New South Wales, Victoria and Western Australia and the peak year of arrival was 1912. This was a transitional phase in English immigration, with a strong emphasis on rural recruitment in Western Australia and Queensland, but a predominantly urban intake in New South Wales and Victoria. The pre-war English immigrants brought few skills to Australia. Many English industries were at their peak of production and prosperity despite rapidly increasing industrial unrest. In the post-war period English industry went into decline and it was easier to recruit miners and metal workers than before. Recruitment was still easiest in London and the Southeast, but northern industrial and mining areas started looking to Australia by the mid-1920s. This post-war immigration was still working class but was more skilled than the pre-war. Those skills were not, however, in demand after the depression struck in 1929 and many English recent arrivals were left derelict, appealing for help to get back to England and creating much bad publicity for Australia.

There were rather more Scots in the inter-war migration, as Scottish industry was declining. Still, more than three-quarters of the assisted were English, numbering about 165 000 between 1920 and 1929 with the peak in 1926, the year of the British general strike in May and the nine-month-long miner's strike. They came from a wider variety of backgrounds and Australia was now attracting skilled workers. Youth migration for farming was widespread in the 1920s and was organised by the

Big Brother Movement, Dr Barnardo's, the Salvation Army, the Church of England, the Dreadnought Trust and other voluntary societies, with the active support of state and Commonwealth governments. Boys sent out under these schemes were asked whether they had farm experience and 'can you milk?', 'can you plough?' and 'can you handle heavy horses?' on their application forms. Many did not come from rural areas and were trained either at Brandon or Claydon in East Anglia or at Scheyville near Sydney.

As the depression spread, immigrants could be accused of 'taking jobs from Australians' and the largest group of such immigrants were the English recent arrivals. Racism against southern Europeans increased in the 1920s but so did hostility to the 'Poms'. Australian conservatives, who ruled nationally for all but two years between 1918 and 1940, were still strongly oriented towards England as 'home'. But it was not the England from which most of the immigrants came. The idealised Home Counties of the English upper classes were very attractive to the Australian social establishment but unknown and alien to the English immigrants. The lot of many inter-war English migrants was not a happy one. Australia was no longer merely an extension of England, if it had ever been. It was no longer the working man's paradise. It looked down on the working-class English immigrants as unwashed, servile and a threat to employment and working conditions. The only consolation was that it looked down upon everyone else even more.

THE 'TEN POUND TOURISTS': 1947–1972

The United Kingdom Assisted Passage scheme was agreed between Australia and the United Kingdom in 1947. Under it British immigrants, once selected, could come to Australia for ten pounds each, with free passages for their children. While distinct figures were not published, it is probable that at least 75% were English and that this had risen to almost 80% by the 1970s. The Scots continued to be overrepresented, as they had been for more than a century, but the Welsh and the Northern Irish were underrepresented. The largest numbers came from London and the Southeast, passing through interviews at Australia House in the Strand. In the early days of the scheme there was a preference for skilled tradesmen but eventually, with the launching of the Bring out a Briton campaign in 1957, almost anyone who could pass the medical could come out for ten pounds. These were the 'ten pound tourists' who, as one cartoon by Molnar depicted it, could get to Australia more cheaply than they could have a holiday in Brighton. It was amazingly easy to get to Australia in the 1950s and 1960s. Between 1947 and 1971 the English population of Australia increased by 460 000.[2]

By 1965 over 80% of British immigrants were being assisted under various programs. No account was taken of ability to pay or of occupation. Over one-quarter of the assisted in the workforce were in professional, administrative or clerical jobs. Policy was directed towards bringing out entire families and most being assisted were dependants although many wives went into employment after arriving. Migrants could be brought out as Commonwealth nominees, as personal nominees, as industrial recruits, as Bring out a Briton nominees, as relatives of settlers or as 'Nest Egg' settlers who had saved enough for a housing deposit. They came from all parts of Britain but most strongly from the metropolitan and suburban areas of London, Manchester and Glasgow.

Because it seemed so easy for the 'ten pound tourists' to get to Australia, there was some local resentment at the 'grumbling Poms' who made their grievances known through the press and often went back to England and did the same. By the 1960s there was concern that the English might not be attracted in such large numbers as before. Italian and Greek immigration was growing, there was full employment in England and living standards were rising to the point where British Prime Minister Harold Macmillan could declare that 'you never had it so good'. The main attractions of Australia for the English seem to have had little to do with direct economic motivations; nor did the main grievances. A small survey of English immigrants, most of them living in Melbourne hostels, found in 1965 that very few had come because of the prospect of better employment or of better living standards. Greater opportunities, especially for the children, were most commonly stressed. England was seen as perfectly comfortable but not offering much in the way of promotion or much possibility of leaving the working class. In an ageing society, many higher positions were held by those older than the typical immigrant. In overcrowded cities there was little chance of enjoying life and the weather was awful. Those features of Australia which were most admired were the climate, the spaciousness and the accessibility of the beach and countryside, the friendliness of the people and the 'way of life'. In contrast to Italian and Greek immigrants, who were very impressed by full employment and high wages, the British respondents attached little significance to economic benefits.[3]

In a major book published in 1973, Alan Richardson, studied the psychology and degree of assimilation of British immigrants, including those who eventually left Australia.[4] He concluded that the majority remain 'recognisably non-Australian throughout their lives' and that 'full assimilation . . . is relatively infrequent for adult members of the generation that first arrives in the host country'. This did not necessarily matter, as after between seven and ten years the immigrant should become stably adjusted with a combination of Australian and English attitudes and identifications. From a longitudinal survey conducted in 1959, 1961 and 1966, he found that 67% of husbands and wives were satisfied with life in Australia. However, only 50% thought they were better off financially and only 45% thought their working conditions were better. Fitting his theory of stable adjustment, 62% thought they had not changed to become 'more Australian' and fully 61% of men in 1961 would support a British team in a contest with Australians. The great majority were skilled workers or from families of skilled workers and had the equivalent of a secondary modern education, the norm for the English. In general, over the period when English immigration was at its height, the respondents were still English in identification, were not remarkably better off, but were quite happy with their decision to emigrate and intended to stay in Australia for the rest of their lives. Of those who decided to leave a rather higher proportion were from the better off sections. Those who had lived in hostels were more likely to leave than those found accommodation by a local sponsor.

Many English arriving during the post-war wave seem to have had limited aspirations. They were often approaching middle age and had higher aspirations for their children than for themselves. The assisted passage schemes favoured family emigration. Little is known about social mobility among

English immigrants but it seems to have been rather slow. Entry into higher education by the children of English immigrants is not remarkable by Australian standards, being very close to the norm and much less than for highly aspiring groups such as Jews or Greeks. The lack of strong economic motivation might be a factor in this easy acceptance of a modest social position. Essentially, those coming out as skilled workers remained at that level and so do most of their children. Those who came out as professionals are also likely to stay at that level. The high proportion of English professionals gives a false impression that the English have 'risen' in society. In most cases they have improved their general situation without changing their class. English workers were more likely to have trade certificates than the Australian-born but were otherwise very similar in their educational attainments.

NO LONGER PRIVILEGED: 1972 TO THE PRESENT

By 1966 about 23% of assisted British migrants were returning home. Between 1971 and 1981 the number of English in Australia increased by only 47 000 and then started to go into a slight decline. In the previous decade the English total had peaked at six times that level. The typical English Australian by the 1980s had lived in Australia for over twenty years and was already middle aged. Australian attempts to attract the English became much less vigorous. The Whitlam government (1972–75) cut the immigrant intake drastically. In 1982 the Fraser Liberal government abolished assisted passages. The English continued to be the largest group arriving in Australia but they were no longer effectively replacing those going home or dying. The windows in the Strand emphasised Australian industry and products rather than the attractions of migration.

Of those emigrating from Britain to Australia between 1975 and 1981 (166 786 in all), 81.5% were from England, with males in a clear majority (56%). The great majority (72%) were in the working ages between fifteen and sixty-five years old, with the greatest numbers between the ages of twenty-five and forty-four. As in nearly all previous English immigrations, the largest proportion came from London and the Southeast, making up 44% of the total. The only other major regions were the Northwest (Liverpool, Manchester and Lancashire) and Yorkshire and Humberside. Over 40% of the Southeasterners came from outside London, from the most prosperous and expansive region of the United Kingdom. There is no evidence that large numbers of the English were escaping from unemployment in the industrial regions, which had risen to record post-war heights during this period.

A high proportion of emigrants were from the professional classes. Those coming from the Southeast counted nearly one-third of those in the working-age groups as professionals, compared to little over one-quarter from the industrial Northwest and slightly less from the North (Durham, Northumberland and Cumberland). The Scottish proportion was one-in-five. Thus English immigrants by the late 1970s were coming to an important extent from the most prosperous region and from the most prestigious occupations.[5] This trend was strengthened by the withdrawal of assisted passages in 1982. English immigration had even less of an economic motivation than ever before.

AREAS OF ENGLISH SETTLEMENT

A consistent English aspiration has been for a respectable suburban existence, not too far from transport and industry and not too deep into the countryside. Each major city has been built up by the addition of suburban belts in which English immigrants have been important but never completely dominant. There have been few 'English' suburbs (or 'Scottish' or 'Irish' suburbs either), simply new areas in which there are large numbers of English settlers. Thus in the build up of Newcastle, several outer suburbs had English populations in 1891 making up 20–30% of the total—such as Adamstown (30.6%); Merewether (27.5%); New Lambton (27.5%); and Lambton (23.7%). A similar pattern can be seen in Melbourne and Sydney in 1981 in areas such as Frankston, Croydon, Knox, Berwick, Campbelltown, and Penrith. This is repeated in Perth in Stirling, Wanneroo, Gosnells, Armadale and Kalamunda and in Adelaide in Elizabeth, Salisbury, and Tea Tree Gully. In 1986 British and Irish-born made up 16% of the population of Perth and 12.5% of the Adelaide total. A preference for suburban life was already established in England by the mid nineteenth century. In contrast to Scottish or European cities, the major English towns grew on the basis of individual homes and gardens, a pattern which completely dominated Australian urban growth.

There were few examples in colonial Australia of towns being settled predominantly from England, in contrast to Christchurch, New Zealand. Sydney had a substantial Irish population; Melbourne, Scots and Irish; Adelaide, Cornish and Germans. In their early days Hobart and Perth were largely English but Brisbane always had an Irish and a German presence. In more recent years, the most concentrated areas of English working-class settlement were in the satellite towns to the south of Fremantle, such as Kwinana, Rockingham and Mandurah, and in the public housing estates north and south of Adelaide, at Elizabeth and Noarlunga.

The lifestyle in such estates may be very similar to that left behind in England. The creation of 'English' institutions, such as the Rose and Crown pub at Elizabeth, and the pursuit of English pastimes, such as darts or soccer, is most marked in these areas. Indeed, in terms of concentration by a particular ethnic group, they are the nearest to 'ghettos' which exist in Australia, although rarely criticised as such. With over 30 000 English born in the Salisbury–Elizabeth–Munno Para area of South Australia there really is a 'Little England' planted in Australia. But it is the England of housing estates and industrial workers, not of country lanes and yeoman farmers.

English industrial workers, mostly assisted to emigrate in the 1950s and 1960s, are concentrated in the areas around Perth and Adelaide already surveyed; around Dandenong in Melbourne; in Wollongong and Shellharbour; to the far west and southwest of Sydney; to the far south of Melbourne; and on the northern and southern outskirts of Brisbane. There are few English-born in provincial cities or country towns other than some exceptions in Western and South Australia such as Albany, Port Hedland and Gawler and in the Latrobe Valley industrial area of Victoria. At least half of post-war English migrants were middle-class and they are concentrated in the major cities. Initially favouring rented accommodation in areas like St Kilda or North Sydney, the middle class English later settled in privately developed outer suburbs. These include Manly and Mosman in Sydney; Croydon, Lilydale, Werribee, the Mornington peninsula and the Dandenongs around Melbourne; Tea Tree Gully, Brighton and Glenelg in Adelaide; and Stirling, Wanneroo, Gosnells, Armadale and

Canning in Perth. Of course, English immigrants who span all classes and age groups may be found anywhere in Australia and there are few, if any, local authority areas which do not have at least a handful who were born in England. But the really large concentrations are in peripheral housing estates or in affluent outer suburbs. These replicate in many respects the kind of areas to which large numbers of the English have been moving within England itself. Their life is very private, being centred on the home. Some of the working-class estates show signs of stress through isolation and juvenile delinquency. But most of the English have found what they seek — comfort and security in a warm climate.

THE ENGLISH IN THE 1980s

In 1981 the number of English-born in Australia was higher than ever before, at 889 124. This had dropped slightly to 880 890 at the next Census in 1986, which was still more than at any time before 1981. The English made up 78.5% of all those born in the United Kingdom and Ireland and this proportion rose to 82% in Western Australia and South Australia. The English were greatly overrepresented in those two states. In Western Australia there were twice as many as the national distribution of population might suggest (17.2% of all English as against 8.7% as the state proportion of the Australian total). In South Australia there were one-and-a-half times as many (14% as against 8.8%).

The English-born population in 1981 did not differ very markedly from other Australians. It was rather older, with a mean age of forty-five as against forty-two for all adults over sixteen. It was more likely to be married (66% of adults against 61%) and very slightly more likely to be male. The average length of residence was twenty years, as the bulk had arrived in the 1960s and there were still some left over from the 1920s. The English, despite their strong position in the professions, had only attended school for a few months more than the average Australian (10.9 years against 10.7) but only 23% had been educated in Australia. This level of education gave them almost exactly the same salary levels and occupational status as the average. In 1981 English family income was $16 749 and the national average $16 490. On a scale of occupational prestige developed at the Australian

National University those in employment scored 36.6, only slightly higher than the norm of 36. The only important respect in which the English differed was that 10.3% lived in rural areas, as against 13.4% of all Australians. Therefore, fewer were engaged in agriculture.[6]

By 1981 the English were not only 'culturally assimilated' but also 'structurally assimilated'—not significantly differing from the average in social terms. They were even closer to the norm than the Scots (fewer of whom lived in rural areas), the Welsh (who had more men than women) or the Northern Irish (very few of whom lived in rural areas). They also earned more than them, on a family income basis. The southern Irish, in contrast to the nineteenth century, were rather better educated on average in terms of years, and had a very slightly higher family income. As might be expected, all four British groups were quite close together and all four favoured Western and South Australia more than the average as places to live. They contrasted with those from other English-speaking backgrounds, such as Americans, Canadians, South Africans, Indians and Sri Lankans, who were better educated and in more prestigious and better paid jobs on average. They were closer to New Zealanders, although these favoured Queensland and New South Wales to a greater degree and were younger. The main contrast was with immigrants from the Mediterranean area, the Middle East and Latin America, who were predominantly in the manual working class. The English were spread over all occupations and areas, as they had been since the founding of modern Australia. Their qualifications, whether academic or trade, were readily acceptable and even sought after. They were not, however, very anxious to become Australian citizens, seeing little need until changes in legislation introduced in 1984. Then they began applying in large numbers, secure in the knowledge that as 'patrials' they and their children still enjoyed the right to enter and live in England whenever they chose. Despite the disappearance of special privileges for British subjects, a majority of eligible British-born immigrants had not taken out Australian citizenship by 1990.

CHAPTER SIX

POPULATE OR PERISH: POST-WAR IMMIGRATION

*A*ll immigration from outside the United Kingdom and other English-speaking countries such as New Zealand, Canada or the United States, had been discouraged during the first 150 years of Australian colonisation. Exceptions were made, especially in Queensland, for 'Nordic racial cousins' between the 1870s and 1914. The British royal family was of direct German origin and racial theories developed in the second half of the nineteenth century argued for the close affinity of the English, German and Scandinavian peoples. Australians were familiar with English history and thus with the historic fact that the 'Anglo-Saxon race', as it was often called in public speeches and school texts, was of Nordic and Germanic origin. The developing concept of an 'Australian race' was based on such ideas, as was the White Australia Policy. The ideal type of an Australian was of English culture and Nordic racial origin. Many went further and argued that the Protestant religion was also central, but that large part of the population who were of Irish Catholic origin naturally resisted this argument. Such ideas did not develop in isolation in Australia but formed part of a general racial theory which was widely accepted throughout the British empire.

Methods of controlling the racial and ethnic character of the Australian people included: outright prohibition of non-Europeans under the White Australia policy and by the operation (though not the wording) of the *Immigration Restriction Act* of 1901; the limitation of assisted passages to British subjects of European race and United Kingdom origin; the introduction of quotas (as in the 1920s) or virtual prohibitions (as in the 1930s) on non-British immigration; the restriction of citizenship rights to British subjects; an official and popular climate of opinion which discouraged 'alien' settlement; and the absence of any effective restrictions on the settlement of British subjects of European origin. Apart from temporary restrictions, such as the banning of German immigration between 1914 and 1925, European aliens were not normally excluded altogether. There was substantial settlement of southern Europeans in the mid-1920s, caused largely by the introduction of quotas for entry to the United States. But this settlement was not welcomed and migrants were made to feel isolated and unwanted, thus limiting the likelihood of them encouraging others to come to Australia. Racist and xenophobic views were openly expressed by public figures, major organisations and the media.

This atmosphere characterised most of the first half of the twentieth century. While small communities of Jews, Italians, Greeks, Germans, Chinese, Maltese and Croatians were able to sustain themselves, they were normally very self-effacing and unobtrusive. The most cosmopolitan situation was on the north Queensland canefields but there were also some inner areas of Sydney, Melbourne and Brisbane with ethnic minorities and some agricultural settlement along the Murray and Murrumbidgee and in Western Australia, especially by Italians. These exceptions to the general rule of British Australia often attracted media hostility. Trade unions introduced membership quotas, especially on the canefields, and the Labor Party was certainly no more tolerant of aliens than its conservative opponents. Thus it is rather surprising, in historical retrospect, that it was a Labor government which introduced mass non-British immigration in 1947 and began the process which changed Australia from a monocultural to a multicultural society over the following forty years.

The post-Second World War immigration program began in an exceptional atmosphere of reform and reconstruction, which influenced Australia as it did other societies emerging from the war. It was believed that Australia was too thinly populated and too reliant on primary industry, to resist attack or invasion from Asia. It must 'populate or perish', a theme which goes back to the previous century though given greater force by the threat of Japanese invasion. While its economy had often provided a very high standard of living, Australia had been shown in the 1890s and the 1930s to be very vulnerable to world market forces and to need adaptation and diversification. Large-scale public works, such as the creation of hydro-electric and irrigation schemes or the modernisation of the road and rail systems, could not be completed without more labour. Primary agricultural and mining industries were also periodically short of labour, which was concentrated in the capital cities and unwilling to move. The post-war Labor government of Chifley was determined to use its powers to change Australian society rapidly and it saw mass migration as one means of doing so. At the same time there was considerable pressure to emigrate from war-ravaged Europe, including Britain.

The original concept of mass migration, as enunciated by public figures, was to return to the British-based programs of the years before and after the First World War. These depended on assisted passages and on the long historical and cultural links built up between Britain and Australia. They also depended (and this presented problems) on mass long-term unemployment in Britain, which had disappeared during the war and was not to return until the 1980s. Although housing conditions and wages were much better in Australia, an important incentive to leave Britain had been reduced by full employment. Moreover, the British Labour government was also engaged in post-war reconstruction and in expanding welfare provision, thus limiting the counterattractions of Australia still further. An important limitation in the first post-war years was a world shortage of passenger shipping suitable for moving civilian migrants used to modest comfort.

The post-war programs continued to stress British migration, and the British were by far the largest recipients of assisted passages for the next thirty years. But most British migration was on a family basis and to the large cities. It did not create a mobile workforce ready to engage in construction, primary industry or even newly expanded factory work. Migrants expected a reasonable standard of housing and there was much discontent with the former army camps into which British settlers were put in the absence of conventional housing. Despite a continuing gap between British and Australian living standards and expectations, most British migrants came from conditions which were not intolerable and expected even better standards on their arrival.

An immediate solution to these problems, and one seized on by Australia as also by Canada and the United States, was presented by the Displaced Persons camps of central Europe which were filled with those uprooted from their homelands by war and unwilling to return to areas now under Soviet occupation. While many DPs were of Slav rather than Nordic origin, they conformed to the idea of assimilability which had developed over the past century. They were fairhaired and fairskinned, most were Catholics or Protestants, many were well educated and young and all were very anxious to escape from the camps and to recreate their lives. Despite some initial fears about the introduction of large numbers of aliens, the Chifley government went ahead with mass recruitment from the camps under the personal supervision of Australia's first minister for immigration, Arthur Calwell.[1]

Calwell's policies were radical and innovative, but were still strongly influenced by consensual views on race, ethnicity and assimilation. Jewish refugees were actively discouraged in the early post-war stages, reflecting a fear of anti-semitism in Australia. 'Former enemies' such as Germans and Italians were specifically prohibited although many who came from eastern Europe had actively supported the Axis cause, an important reason for not wishing to return to the Soviet bloc. Allied refugees of Asian origin, thousands of whom had fled to Australia from the Japanese, were deported under legislation introduced by Calwell in 1946. Thus the DP program was innovatory in bringing in large numbers of non-British aliens, but conservative in terms of adhering strictly to the White Australia Policy.

The importance of the DP program in ultimately changing the ethnic character of Australia cannot be underestimated. It was assumed by Calwell and his colleagues that Europeans would assimilate rapidly and become 'New Australians', a term revived from the 1920s when it had been applied to British migrants. An Assimilation Branch was created within the Department of Immigration to pursue this objective. At the same time it was wisely acknowledged that there were problems in settling a relatively large number of newcomers about whom Australians knew nothing. The post-war refugee program, which ran from 1947 to 1953, led to several innovations which were to be developed for subsequent immigrant waves from outside the United Kingdom. These included: English-language teaching; welfare programs for migrants;

public relations campaigns favouring ethnic tolerance; public support for immigration and immigrants from politicians, important individuals and organisations; the expansion of the Immigration Department into settlement and citizenship services beyond its original brief of recruiting newcomers; and the extension of assisted passages to non-British immigrants.

These new developments were inhibited until the 1970s by the assimilationist hopes of public authorities, which were gradually abandoned as unrealistic. But they were very important in clearing the way for the next stage of mass immigration —the attraction of large numbers of Europeans through assisted passages and intergovernment agreements. Never before had Australia committed itself to massive expenditure on the deliberate introduction of non-British migrants, nor to agreements with governments other than that of the United Kingdom to bring out and provide for non-British subjects.

As refugees, the Displaced Persons were willing to accept conditions which would have been rejected by voluntary migrants. They were transported in troop carriers, the first of which, the *General Heintzelman*, arrived in Fremantle in November 1947. They were housed in former army camps, the most famous of which, Bonegilla, did not close until 1971. They were allocated to work for two years which they had to accept on pain of deportation but which was paid for at standard trade union rates. Families were divided as many men were sent to all-male construction sites in areas like the Snowy Mountains. The labour force created was completely mobile but also completely unskilled as nearly all men were classified as 'labourers' and women as 'domestics', recalling the terms used for so many assisted British immigrants in the previous century. The benefits for DPs included food and lodging, guaranteed employment and English language teaching. The memories of post-war refugees are very ambivalent, combining gratitude at rescue from Europe with resentment at exploitation by the Australian authorities. But the greatest resentments were often caused by public attitudes, including the expectation that new arrivals would not speak foreign languages in public and would strive to appear identical to native Australians, which most found difficult. Subsequent reaction against assimilationism was often led by eastern Europeans who had passed through these experiences.

The major ethnic minorities created in Australia by the

post-War DP program include Poles, the first of whom went to work on Tasmanian hydro-electric schemes in September 1947; Estonians, Latvians and Lithuanians, collectively known as 'Balts' and first arriving on the *General Heintzelman*, selected by Calwell as young and blonde; Ukrainians, Croatians, Hungarians, Czechs and Russians. Passengers on the *General C. H. Muir*, arriving in Melbourne in October 1950, classified themselves as: 525 Yugoslavs, 443 Poles, ninety-five Latvians, fifty-four Hungarians, forty-five Czechoslovaks, twenty-six Ukrainians, twenty-three Estonians, nineteen Romanians, nineteen Russians, thirteen Bulgarians, eight Germans, seven Lithuanians and three Georgians, of whom 72% were Catholics.[2] The central point about these nationalities is that they had little or no previous presence in Australia. Few Australians knew anything about their languages, history or cultures.

This presented Australian authorities with the dilemma that they wished the New Australians to assimilate as quickly as possible but had few effective ways of communicating with them or securing their effective entry into Australian life. Once released from their work bonds most settled in the major cities, especially in the outer industrial suburbs which were rapidly expanding to the west of Melbourne, Sydney and Adelaide. They began immediately to form social and self-help clubs, a process which Australians had frequently deplored but which is inevitable and universal for immigrants in an alien culture. Today most of the eastern European communities are quite elderly, as many were not replenished by further immigration. They have, however, been quite successful in handing on their culture and history to their descendants and their organisations and media are still viable forty years after they were first established.

The first wave of post-war non-British immigrants caused few problems for Australia, although they had many problems of their own. They could not return to their homelands for political reasons and this cut off one of the options which southern Europeans had always kept open and sometimes realised. Some tried to become politically active in the anti-communist atmosphere of the 1950s and a few still hold office in the Liberal Party though virtually none have ever been elected to public office. Today opinion polling shows eastern Europeans to be overwhelmingly conservative and anti-Labor in their politics, an attitude compounded by their advancing years which tend to reinforce conservatism. Some of their ethnic communities show signs of 'fossilisation' in preserving loyalties, attitudes and even terminology which have become out of date. Others, such as the Ukrainians and Latvians, have been able to educate their children in their own culture. All are now faced with possibilities closed to them in the past, namely a return to countries freed from communism or the arrival of compatriots as free immigrants from those countries.

The Displaced Persons program was completed by 1953. It opened up the possibility of assisted mass migration from Europe by showing that Australians would not reject such migration if it presented no threat to working conditions or to the total domination of society by those of British and Irish origins. The Good Neighbour movement, which had grown out of the need to settle both British and DP migrants, was an important agency for converting Australians to the desirability of continuing mass migration. Major employers, especially BHP and the motor manufacturers, had found migrants essential to the expansion of their industries, which required a large, mobile and compliant labour force. The housing industry, too, found that British and European building workers were skilled and that migrant families required new housing on the outskirts of the cities, where new industries were also being located. Public works had come to rely heavily on DP labour. Post-war migrants were no longer seen as rural pioneers. Most workable land was already taken up and the employment of refugees as rural labourers proved to be only transient.

The second stage of post-war immigration rested on two bases. One was the continuing attraction of British migrants through assisted passages, as for the previous century. The other was the extension of those passages to non-British and the easing of restrictions on alien settlement. While it was not clearly spelled out, the objective of mass immigration in the 1950s and 1960s was to create a larger labour force which could help to expand manufacturing industry. Looking at the post-war experience of Germany and other European economies, Australian population planners saw relatively unskilled workers from rural and provincial backgrounds as a potential urban workforce. European population movement was driven by post-war disruption, by the demands of industry and by rural depopulation. Only a fragment of those on the move chose Australia, but this choice was encouraged by assistance with passage money and with settlement. It was diverted from the United States which still maintained effective nationality quotas against southern Europeans.

The post-war second wave from Europe consisted largely of those seeking better conditions and full employment. They were not necessarily seeking permanent residence in Australia, as official policy desired. Southern European traditions encouraged the notion of living away from home for many years, bringing out wives or fiancées when it became financially possible and then returning with savings to the native village for retirement. As in America in the past, this pattern was often hard to maintain. Many of those intending to return home never did so, especially as their native villages became depopulated or fell behind the rising standards of their homelands. Children born in Australia were reluctant to 'return' to countries of which they knew little. The major immigration of the 1950s and 1960s built communities of Italians, Greeks, Maltese, Croatians, Macedonians and eventually Turks in the working-class suburbs of major cities which were much larger than anything experienced by urban Australia in the past. In contrast to the pre-war situation, these communities were large and varied enough to provide a complete life, to support media, social and sporting clubs and religious institutions. Eventually they began to have an impact on the voting rolls of Labor politicians and to establish links with the Labor and trade union movements which were to last into the present.

Immigration in this second wave was largely controlled through government-to-government agreements. In the past these had only been contracted with the British government, for example under the *Empire Settlement Act* of 1922. The terms under which immigrants would be assisted were spelled out and most agreements also indicated a responsibility to find work and extend social security in Australia. This was relatively easy to guarantee, as unemployment levels rarely exceeded 2% of the workforce before the 1970s. The first agreement, unsurprisingly, was with the British government in 1946, following precedents which were over a century old. The next, in 1948, was with the British colony of Malta. Other agreements in 1947 extended assisted passages to allied ex-service personnel and formalised arrangements with the International Refugee Organization.

For the next twenty years there was a spate of inter-government agreements designed to assist non-British immigration. Such agreements were made with the Netherlands and Italy in 1951, with West Germany, Austria and Greece in 1952, with Finland, Switzerland, Sweden, Denmark and Norway in 1954, with Spain in 1958, with Turkey in 1968 and with Yugoslavia in 1970. The form of these agreements varied and some were renegotiated as conditions changed. The Italian government became increasingly concerned about the social and economic situation of Italian immigrants, especially after riots at the Bonegilla reception camp in 1961. The Greek government complained in 1965 about the recruitment of single girls as domestic servants, an echo of the nineteenth century. The arrangements made were not uniform and preferences were clearly expressed for immigrants considered to be assimilable. In 1959, the minister for immigration (A. Downer) told the citizenship convention that 'Holland is one of the few countries in Europe with people to export of a type that can quickly merge with the Australian community'.[3] The level of assistance offered varied by country, being greatest for the Scandinavian countries, the Netherlands, Germany and, of course, Britain. The majority of southern Europeans, other than Maltese, financed their own voyages, often through borrowing from relatives for whom they agreed to work after arrival. This contributed to the concentration of Greeks and Italians in certain suburbs and occupations.

Immigration from continental Europe reflected social, economic and political conditions, all of which improved very rapidly from the early 1950s. Free movement of labour within western Europe became much easier with the creation of the European Economic Community under the 1957 Treaty of Rome. Most non-British immigration was characterised by rapid rises to a peak, followed by steady decline to a minimal level by the early 1970s. The number of Italian-born in Australia (at 289 476) was highest in 1971, having more than doubled since 1954. The number of Greek-born (at 160 200) was also highest in 1971, having increased six-fold since 1954. The Dutch peaked even earlier (at 102 083) in 1961, doubling in numbers since 1954 but increasing fifty-fold since 1947. German-born, some of them Displaced Persons, were steadier at a level of about 110 000 between 1961 and 1986. Numbers from Scandinavia were always small, as these countries had not been severely affected by the war and had higher real incomes than Australia. The largest numbers came from Finland (which was war affected) but these also peaked in 1971 at 10 359 residents.

The poorer countries of Europe, especially those outside the European Community, were still showing an interest in migrating in the 1970s. But this was very modified by their access to the growing labour markets of Germany, Switzerland and France and by the ending of the United States national quota system in 1965. These changes particularly affected migration from southern Italy, Greece and Yugoslavia. However, Yugoslav migration to Australia held steady into the 1980s, shifting its focus towards the poorer southern districts and especially Macedonia.

The strategy of attracting immigrants and labour from 'assimilable' sources and from industrial and urban societies was failing by the early 1970s, though British immigration continued high and the numbers of English-born did not reach their greatest height (at 889 124) until 1981. Apart from declining arrivals, there was a growing rate of return to countries like Germany, Britain and the Netherlands and to the more prosperous areas of Italy. Some temporary and exceptional boosts were given by special arrangements and by refugee situations. Spanish rural workers were recruited for the sugar industry under the agreement of 1958, but this flow was also affected by free movement within Europe which attracted many Spanish workers to France. The Turkish inflow after 1968 raised Turkish-born numbers to more than 30 000, but this intake produced many social problems, including high rates of illiteracy and unemployment and low levels of citizenship. Two major refugee intakes followed the Hungarian revolution of 1956 and the Soviet intervention in Czechoslovakia in 1968.

By the time that the Whitlam government drastically reduced assisted numbers in 1974 and 1975, Australia was mainly attracting immigrants from the poorest countries of Europe (such as Yugoslavia, Turkey or Portugal) and from the poorest regions within southern European countries (such as Calabria or Macedonia). These immigrants were mainly going into manufacturing industry and settling in the industrial suburbs of Melbourne, Adelaide, Wollongong, Sydney and Geelong. The demand for industrial labour continued to expand and much of it was semi-skilled. The huge intake of immigrants also fuelled the construction industry, where many workers were also immigrants. Some went into mining, particularly at Mount Isa and the Pilbara. But rural recruitment was very limited and some major employers of immigrant labour in the past, most notably the sugar canefields, became mechanised. Italians and Dutch were well represented in rural Australia (though in different areas) but most new arrivals settled in the major industrial centres.

European settlement in the second post-war wave was essentially concentrated between 1952 and 1972. Migration from Yugoslavia or Turkey continues into the present, with some interest from Germany, but often from single men rather than families. The social and occupational patterns created in that period still remain important. While migrants settled widely, they created suburbs and shopping centres on which their imprint is still very visible. The largest numbers came from Italy, particularly from Calabria, Sicily and Abruzzo. Their initial settlement was in inner-city areas such as Leichhardt in Sydney and Carlton in Melbourne. This was a transitory phase which has left major commercial centres behind. Southern Europeans have been especially likely to buy their own homes and this has taken them further out in the major cities. By the 1980s the major centres of Italian settlement were in the Sydney inner west (Drummoyne and Concord) and outer west (Liverpool); in northern Melbourne (Coburg, Brunswick and Preston); in northeast Adelaide (Payneham); and in Fremantle. While Italians were predominantly industrial and construction workers, many of their children were passing into the middle classes. The Italian greengrocer, the stereotype of the pre-war immigrant, was no longer typical, though southern Italians were still very important in the fruit and vegetable industries at all levels from growing to retailing.

Greeks also began their residence in the inner suburbs and were as concentrated in industry as the Italians. They too have produced a middle class and second generation university entry is at a higher level than for most ethnic groups. Consequently there are Greek populations in such affluent suburbs as Doncaster and Malvern in Melbourne. Melbourne is often claimed as the 'third most Greek city in the world' (which is probably no longer true since mass Greek migration to New York and Chicago). It is certainly the most Greek city in Australia, with large communities in the Richmond, Prahran, Oakleigh and Northcote areas. In Sydney, Greek settlement is more concentrated around a core in Marrickville extending to Maroubra and Canterbury. Greeks in Brisbane have a heavy concentration in inner-city West End and are similarly strong in inner-city Thebarton in Adelaide. In contrast to the Italians, there is almost no major Greek rural settlement.

The other southern European communities are smaller and less noticeable than the Italians and Greeks. Maltese have mainly settled in the scattered western industrial suburbs of Melbourne (Sunshine and St Albans) and Sydney (Blacktown and Holroyd). They are predominantly industrial and transport workers and have not created commercial centres. Yugoslavs, Turks, Portuguese and Spanish-speakers (mostly from Latin America) tend to be found in similar industrial areas. These are now mainly in such outer suburbs as Fairfield in Sydney or Sunshine and Broadmeadows in Melbourne. There are southern European concentrations in Wollongong and Adelaide but a more scattered settlement pattern in Perth and Brisbane. The numerical importance of the 'second wave' European migrants has put their communities and organisations at the centre of the debate on multiculturalism. Most were not proficient in English and many have never learnt the language as they arrived at a time when English-language tuition was ineffective. In the absence of the settlement services available for many refugees, and arriving without assistance, the European immigrants were able to assist each other through organisations formed from their own resources. The Italian and Greek media expanded rapidly and gave cohesion to what might otherwise have been a disoriented population. Most European arrivals between the 1950s and the 1970s went into industry, bought their own homes in working-class suburbs and aimed at improving the social standing of their children. They were a dynamic influence on Australian growth. Eventually those who had not returned home became Australian citizens. Their presence could not be ignored in the major cities, the unions or the educational and welfare systems.

'Second wave' immigration was effectively over by 1975, though the communities created are still a major component of the Australian population. Attempts to recruit from Latin America or from the 'mixed race' minorities of Asia were inspired by the high return rates and the low recruitment rates noticeable by the mid-1960s. But after 1975 the emphasis inevitably shifted towards societies closer to Australia, less prosperous and more politically disturbed than Europe. A higher level of unemployment and the decline of the manu-facturing workforce made the strategy of attracting unskilled labour less sensible than it had been while secondary industry was expanding. Clothing, textiles and footwear, which employed thousands of immigrant women, were all in decline. The importance of the second wave was in creating large and viable communities of non-English-speaking Australians and in showing that less assimilable migrants could settle very successfully and without social friction. By 1975 the non-British component of Australian society had became too large to be ignored.

CHAPTER SEVEN

THE END OF WHITE AUSTRALIA

*A*ustralia became internationally famous for its exclusion of non-Europeans but 'White Australia' effectively lasted as an administrative policy with widespread popular support for less than ninety years. The term was first used in the early 1880s, probably in articles by William Lane. It was taken up by the populist *Bulletin*, which kept the slogan 'Australia for the White Man' on its masthead until 1961, when it was removed by its new editor, Donald Horne.

The forces which sustained White Australia included the Australian Labor Party, which enshrined the maintenance of racial purity in its first national platform of 1906. The party's largest affiliate, the Australian Workers' Union, had a similar objective and was particularly important in determining the ethnic composition of the rural workforce in Queensland. Radical unions, such as the Seamen's Union, later became more sympathetic towards Asians, provided that they did not compete unfairly with white Australians. Under the influence of the Communist Party, which was at its height in the 1940s, union enthusiasm for White Australia began to wane. By the 1960s the pre-eminence of the Australian Workers' Union was also waning until today its influence is relatively unimportant outside Queensland and rural New South Wales. Strong support for White Australia came from the Returned Services' League, but that too faced declining numbers and influence by the 1960s. The major conservative parties, the Liberals and the Country Party (now the Nationals), both supported existing policy, but with increasing reservations among the Liberals after the retirement of Sir Robert Menzies in 1966.

As long as White Australia was concerned with preventing unskilled Asian labour from reducing the gains of unionised Australians, it had a wide appeal. Its basis in racist theory, which gave it force from the 1880s to the 1940s, became increasingly discredited among the well educated. In its most strident form, Australian racism argued that Asians and other non-Europeans (including especially Aborigines) were genetically inferior and would only debase the existing population if allowed to intermarry and produce children. As this process was already far advanced in many Aboriginal populations and seemingly irreversible, assimilationists shifted the argument towards 'saving' those of mixed race, if necessary by removing them from their families and communities.

For immigrants, however, the problem could be more easily solved simply by refusing entry, especially to women or to close relatives of those already present. Thus the deliberate intention was that the larger non-European populations (mainly Aboriginal and Chinese) would die out within a generation and that no other similar communities could form. These objectives appeared close to achievement in 1947, when the Census showed only 25 000 'Asians' and 87 000 Aborigines in a population of over 7 million.

However, the racist claims of genetic inferiority were brought into intellectual disrepute by the collapse of Nazism as a system and an ideology in 1945. By the 1960s significant numbers of Asian students were studying at Australian universities and the economic rise of Japan was already being acknowledged. Arguments which had been widely accepted in the 1930s were completely unacceptable thirty years later. The case for White Australia rested increasingly on references to labour competition, to potential social tension and to the possibility of dual loyalties were Australia to be involved in conflict in the Asian region. These arguments were expedient and pragmatic and lacked the bite of previous positions based on racial and genetic theories.

The administration of White Australia became increasingly absurd and incompatible with planned mass immigration. In the late 1940s the Calwell administration had been able to return Asian wartime refugees to their homelands and to prevent the arrival of Japanese and other Asian spouses, though not without protest from Christian groups and from one of the few independent Asian states, the Philippines. Cases of exclusion and deportation became increasingly controversial by the 1960s. Two influential instances were the exclusion of a young Fiji Indian girl, Nancy Prasad, in 1965, and the attempted deportation of two Darwin Malay divers in 1961. Media treatment of these cases was sympathetic to the victims and they were supported by some churches, by unionists and by students. Opposition to White Australia grew amongst student activists, especially in Melbourne, and became less unpopular in the ALP and its affiliated unions, despite the resistance of the party leader, Calwell.

By the 1960s the great majority of Asians were living under independent governments who would not accept exclusion of their citizens based on ideas of racial inferiority. The United States was unwilling to allow migrant recruitment while Australia excluded black Americans. Black British were also increasing in numbers with immigration from the West Indies and southern Asia. There were cases of them being denied the assisted passages available readily to other British citizens, although no evidence that the British government objected publicly to this discrimination.

Perhaps the most important factor in abandoning White Australia and refusing to return to it has been the need to consolidate international relationships in the Asia–Pacific region. While many Asian countries, such as Japan or Singapore, have very rigorous immigration programs of their own, they are also densely populated. The movement of goods, capital, tourists and labour in the Asia–Pacific region affects Australia. The conduct of friendly international and trading relationships prohibits any entry policy based on racial discrimination. Already by the 1950s Australian foreign ministers were being questioned on their overseas visits and were forced into stating that 'there was no White Australia Policy', which all informed opinion knew to be untrue.

The most important factor in ending non-European exclusion was foreign policy considerations. The objective of sustaining a mass immigration of skilled workers and their families was also contradicted by the exclusion of otherwise acceptable immigrants on racial grounds. Important communities of European culture and descent were leaving independent Asian states in the 1960s. Most sought to return to the colonial metropolis, which they had been taught to think of as 'home' even when they had never been there. Such communities included the Sir Lankan Burghers, the Anglo-Indians, Dutch and French Eurasians, Anglo-Burmese and other predominantly Christian communities. With the coming of independence they often lost the relatively privileged position which they had previously enjoyed. But most were of mixed European and Asian descent and were not always acceptable in Australia because of their appearance, which was frequently their only 'Asian' characteristic. Another category who would have been acceptable were it not for racial exclusion were the so-called 'distinguished' Asians, many of them also fluent in English, of Christian religion and culturally attuned to Western society. While there had always been a concession for visitors and students from the Asian élites, they were not permitted to settle permanently.

The first modifications in the White Australia Policy were designed to assist the settlement of these two categories—the Europeanised minorities and the highly qualified. In 1956 the conditions for entry of 'mixed race' immigrants were relaxed and clarified. At the same time those few remaining wartime refugees were granted permanent residence along with others who had been in Australia for at least fifteen years. Non-Europeans married to white Australians were permitted to apply for citizenship, which had previously been denied. Japanese wives of Australian ex-servicemen had been provisionally admitted for five years in 1952 and this allowed them to become citizens and thus to remain. In the following year the right to apply for citizenship was extended to all other non-Europeans who had been in Australia for fifteen years. This conformed to a view which had been expressed by the courts, that after long residence immigrants had become part of the 'Australian community'. None of these concessions made it easier for immigrants of unmixed Asian descent to enter Australia, although they rationalised the situation of those who had previously settled.

Similar minor concessions were made almost annually in the 1960s in an incrementalist approach which allowed the exclusion policy to be gradually modified without attracting popular opposition or greatly increasing the numbers of non-Europeans admitted. The major beneficiaries in the 1960s were the Asian communities of mixed descent, who settled in Australia in their thousands during the decade. They were, however, culturally much closer to Europeans than to Asians, were fluent in English and formed an active component of

Catholic and Protestant congregations. Many were politically conservative and middle class and they settled in the appropriate residential suburbs, especially in Melbourne and Perth.

In 1959 citizens were allowed to bring non-European spouses and children into Australia, when they were eligible for citizenship and thus for permanent residence. This concession was extended to British citizens in 1960. Further restrictions on those of mixed descent were lifted in 1964, allowing the entry of large numbers of Anglo-Burmese, Anglo-Indians and Sri Lankan Burghers. By this time the Immigration Reform Group in Melbourne had been campaigning against the White Australia Policy for five years. The Liberal and Labor parties removed the phrase from their platforms in 1965. Even so, opponents of White Australia were only campaigning for the end of the principle and the admission of a very small quota of non-Europeans.

The erosion and abolition of the policy took only six years after the retirement of Sir Robert Menzies and of Arthur Calwell, in 1966 and early 1967 respectively. In March 1966 the policy was reviewed and modified, with a reduction of the citizenship eligibility requirement to only five years of residence. In 1967 a migration agreement was concluded with Turkey. This was actively supported by the Returned Services' League and the Turks were regarded as white Europeans (which is how they saw themselves officially). But they were also Muslims and, indeed, still form the largest national component of Australia's Islamic population. Thus if the objection to non-Europeans was cultural and not racial, as many supporters of existing policy claimed, the Turkish migration agreement was inconsistent with such thinking.

It is sometimes claimed that the White Australia Policy effectively ended in 1966. Certainly the basic principle of total exclusion had been steadily eroded over the previous decade. But the open abolition of the policy had to wait for the Whitlam government, which declared in early 1973 that future admissions would be universal in the sense of ignoring race, ethnicity, religion or cultural background. Later in the year the government went further in ending discrimination which had previously favoured British citizens seeking to become naturalised Australians. These changes were consistent with domestic Labor policy, which sought to move against racial discrimination in setting up a Commissioner for Community Relations and passing the *Racial Discrimination Act* of 1975.

The impact of these changes was not apparent at once because the Whitlam government cut the migrant intake altogether. They were resistant to the admission of large numbers of Vietnamese refugees after the fall of Saigon in 1975, although non-Europeans from Timor did arrive in Darwin after the Indonesian invasion and were accepted for permanent residence. The decisive year in the final breakdown of White Australia was essentially 1976. The first Vietnamese 'boat people' arrived in Darwin in April and special concessions were made for those escaping from the civil war which had begun in Lebanon. In contrast to previous Lebanese, who had been Christians, an increasing number of these were Muslims.

Since 1976 the proportion of immigrants which has come from Asia has reached between 35% and 40%, having been negligible before that and largely consisting of those of European culture and descent. In 1988–89, out of 145 000 settler arrivals, 37.6% were from Asia and 5.4% from the Middle East. This contrasted with 19.3% from Britain and Ireland and 10% from Europe. As many came from Malaysia as from the whole of northern Europe and more from the Philippines than from the whole of southern Europe. While the British and New Zealanders still made up the two largest national components, they were outnumbered by Asians. The contrast with previous decades is quite marked. In 1966–67 (effectively the last year of rigid exclusion) the only Asian country among the top ten sources was India (mainly Anglo-Indians) and the only Middle Eastern source was Lebanon (mainly Christians). In 1976–77 (the first year of effective universalisation), Malaysia and the Philippines were already amongst the top ten, together with Lebanon. By 1988–89 Asian top sources included the Philippines, Vietnam, Malaysia, Hong Kong, China, India and Sir Lanka, leaving only the three English-speaking societies, Britain, New Zealand and South Africa among the ten largest sources.

Such a rapid dismantling of a policy which had lasted for two generations and been widely accepted and even praised, naturally provokes a reaction. Yet before discussing the reaction it is worth asking why the shifts have occurred and what their importance might be for the future of Australia. One obvious factor is that once restrictions were removed, many who had links with Australia or who sought to move to an English-speaking country, were able to settle. Most important among these have been immigrants from Malaysia and the Philippines. Contacts with Malaysia were well established through the student intake of the 1960s, while the Catholic religion and English-language education of Filipinos turned their attention towards Australia, which is closer than the United States to which most Filipinos still emigrate. English is the *lingua franca* of large parts of southeast and southern Asia, allowing their educated classes to seek opportunities in Australia, Canada and the United States once entry into Britain became restricted in the 1960s.

Proximity to Australia became important once assisted passages and government-to-government agreements were ended in the early 1980s. Such agreements had all been with European states (including Turkey), the last being with Yugoslavia in 1970. They were designed to regulate the conditions under which Europeans would settle in Australia and became redundant once universalism was proclaimed in 1973. Assisted passages were also designed to control the ethnic character of Australia and had been used for that purpose since the 1830s. By lessening the cost of travel it was possible to attract millions from Britain and Europe. By denying passages to non-Europeans, it was possible to discourage them from coming to Australia, even when they had lived in Europe or North America. The final ending of assisted passages in 1982 abolished an important device for influencing the sources of migrant intake. It made proximity to Australia increasingly important. Not only were fares from Britain and Europe very expensive, but the costs of periodic return to family and friends was also a disincentive.

Undeniably, one of the major factors in the shifting emphasis away from Britain and Europe has been the decline of differentials between Australian and European living standards. As a 'rule of thumb' it has been asserted that a gap of at least 25% in measurable incomes is necessary for mass migration from one country to another to be sustained. That gap has simply disappeared for most of those sources which contributed to Australian population growth in the 1950s and 1960s. Of European states only Britain, Ireland, Yugoslavia, Poland, Germany and Portugal each sent more than 1000 migrants in 1988–89. The British links are long established and historic, with over 1 million British-born currently living in Australia. Germany is the largest European state. Otherwise the sources are amongst the poorest in Europe. There is now almost no sustained movement from such historic sources as Italy, Greece, Malta or the Netherlands. This is not, as some have argued, evidence of discrimination against Europeans, but simply evidence of European prosperity at a level which has ended the incentive to emigrate anywhere. Economic advantage is not the only reason for emigrating, though it is the most obvious. Much post-war emigration from Europe was motivated by social disorder and destruction resulting from the war, which is now only a distant memory.

Immigration of non-Europeans since 1975 has been predominantly from Asia and the Middle East, with small numbers from Latin America, the West Indies, Africa, the Pacific Islands, Britain and the United States. Some major countries of emigration, most notably Bangladesh, have added very few to the Australian population and no permanent immigration officer has been stationed there. Most of those from the Middle East and Latin America would already have been eligible for entry before 1975. Indeed a deliberate campaign of recruitment was started in Latin America in 1970 and the agreement with Turkey had been signed two years before. Lebanese were never regarded as ineligible and small communities of Lebanese Christians were already established in Australia by 1900. What has made the Middle Eastern immigration controversial is not its racial origins but its increasingly Muslim character. Opponents of Asian migration usually include the Middle East in their figures, as does the Australian Bureau of Statistics but not the Department of Immigration. The anomaly of basing entry on race and appearance is well illustrated by the contrast between Latin American and Lebanese immigrants, few of whom could speak English, and Indian and Sir Lankan immigrants, the great majority of whom in the 1970s spoke English fluently and used it as their home language.

The motivation of Asian immigrants has varied as much as that of previous European arrivals, as have their characteristics and experiences. The largest numbers have come either from the former British empire (mainly Burma, Malaysia, India, Sri Lanka, Singapore and Hong Kong), from the former American colony of the Philippines or from the Indo-Chinese war zone. Those born in former British Asian colonies numbered 171 687 in 1986, or 42% of all Australians born in Asia other than the Middle East. The great majority were fluent in English and many were from the professional and clerical classes both in their homelands and in Australia. Consequently they have generally been better educated than the Australian average and have more prestigious and better paid jobs. They have few of the characteristics of the Asians who were migrating to Australia before the adoption of the White Australia Policy. They are culturally much closer to the Australian norm than most of the Europeans who arrived in the 1950s and 1960s, especially in their mastery of English and in their educational background. They have settled in middle-class suburban areas of Melbourne, Perth and Sydney, with considerable temporary settlement by students near some of the major universities. The middle-class emigration from countries where the élites have been educated in English continues, and is even more marked than in Canada and the United States. In 1988–89 new settlers born in former British Asian colonies numbered 23 365, or 43% of those coming from Asia to Australia.

While not all those arriving from British-influenced areas are necessarily assimilated to British culture, those of middle-class background frequently are. With the exhaustion of the sources of mixed race migrants by the late 1970s, an increasing number are likely to be Muslim, Hindu or Buddhist rather than Christian and to be fluent in an Asian language (which many of those who came before the abolition of White Australia were not). The tendency to come from the former British empire is also apparent for those from other continents. Of African arrivals in 1988–89, 79% were from former British territories, as were nearly all those from Oceania. Free movement within the empire, which had been upheld by the British in the nineteenth century, no longer holds and is no longer British policy. However the importance of historic and cultural ties is still very relevant in attracting non-European immigrants to Australia, many of them well educated. Such historic ties have been important throughout the history of international migration and are especially relevant for the continuing attraction of large numbers of English-speakers to Australia, even from very prosperous countries like Canada and the United States.

The second important factor in determining migration flows of non-Europeans has been civil and international strife.

Large areas of the world have become characterised by endemic civil disorder, including much of Africa, Latin America, the Middle East and Southeast Asia. States like Sri Lanka and the Philippines, which were previously relatively stable democracies, have in recent years witnessed continuing civil war. Such internal disorder periodically involves international intervention, as in Vietnam and Afghanistan. The consequences of such intervention are usually to escalate conflict and cause massive displacement of civilians. While democracy has been restored in some societies, such as Argentina or Uruguay, it has collapsed in others, such as Fiji. The refugee population of the world, defined as those fleeing from their homelands and temporarily resident elsewhere, equals the population of Australia. However only limited numbers have come to Australia and they have come from a relatively small number of disturbed situations.

Most of those escaping from civil disorder since 1975 have come from the three Indo-Chinese states (Vietnam, Laos and Cambodia) and from Lebanon. The former have mainly arrived as refugees from camps outside Indo-China, while the latter have entered under relaxed rules first implemented in 1976. In 1988–89 Indo-Chinese made up 54% of those settled under refugee and special humanitarian programs, eastern Europeans were 18%, Latin Americans were also 18% and Middle Easterners were 9%. But many others were clearly emigrating because of actual or anticipated problems arising from civil disorder, including 2690 from Fiji, 2937 from Sri Lanka and at least some of the 9204 from the Philippines who arrived in the same period. These are not refugees in any legal sense. While Australia took 1492 from El Salvador, 1217 from Cambodia, 3863 from Vietnam and 475 from the Soviet Union as refugee or humanitarian settlers in 1988–89, it took only twenty-four from Sri Lanka and only two from the whole of Oceania (which includes Fiji).

Thus Australian refugee policy is selective and no attempt is made to service the large numbers of African or Afghan refugees, nor to extend refugee concessions to other disturbed states such as Sri Lanka. The experience of Canada and West Germany has been that refugee numbers can escalate very rapidly. Australia has been very cautious about encouraging the idea that is is a haven for anyone escaping disturbed situations. A responsibility for Indo-Chinese was assumed by the Fraser government as part of the aftermath of the Vietnam war in which Australia took an active part. But most other refugee intake in recent years has been token, from States such as El Salvador, Ethiopia, Romania or Iran. For some years about one-in-ten immigrants admitted have been within the refugee and humanitarian categories. Australia has taken more Vietnamese refugees proportionate to its population than any other State. But such refugee intake is not exceptional when compared with the policy of Canada, the United States, West Germany or the Scandinavian countries.

Apart from the former British empire and disturbed regions, the other major source of non-European immigrants has been the Philippines. A well educated society, with nearly a century of historic links to the United States, predominantly Catholic and with many millions fluent in English, the Philippines has links with several developed countries and is a major source of migrants for the United States, the Persian Gulf and even, in recent years, Japan. Such links were not important with Australia until the ending of the White Australia Policy, but since then there has been rapid increase in Filipino migration to the extent that more than 50 000 Australian residents were Philippines-born by 1990. Filipino settlers, like those from former British colonies, tended to be better educated than the Australian average and to be in better jobs. They also contained a female majority. Many of these were married to Australian men, although the controversial 'mail-order bride' system was finally outlawed by the Philippines government in 1990. Such marriages have been a factor in spreading Filipino settlers throughout Australia, including such remote districts as Mount Isa and Alice Springs. Despite their large numbers, there are few metropolitan concentrations of Filipinos nor have they followed other Asian migrants into the restaurant trade. The great majority are Catholics and have been integrated into the Australian Church through the use of Filipino chaplains in some cases.

Another aspect of Asian migration to Australia has been the relocation of Chinese within the region. As in the nineteenth century, Chinese form the largest non-European group in Australia, other than Aborigines. But migration from China itself has been very limited in recent years and some of it in the 1960s was of Europeans, mainly Russians. The great majority of Chinese in Australia were not born in China but in Southeast Asia. In recent years nationalism has been directed against the Chinese in a number of former colonial societies, including Malaysia, Vietnam and Indonesia. Although very well placed in business and the professions, the Chinese have started to look outside Asia for relocation. A strong movement has been generated by the impending absorption of Hong Kong into China in 1997. Thus Chinese emigration is prompted not by economic necessity but by fear of further restrictions on business enterprise and on Chinese language and culture. Forced assimilation, restrictions on entry to education and government service, taxes and even expropriations have faced the various Overseas Chinese communities since the 1940s. Many are now moving to Canada, the United States and Australia. Chinese have been particularly important in the business migration programs of Canada and Australia, forming 80% of the Australian intake in recent years. More than 1% of the Australian population are now of substantially Chinese origin. This is five times the level of the 1940s, but only one-third the level of the 1850s. However, they do not come directly from China. Only with the temporary acceptance of over 20 000 Chinese students resident in Australia in 1990 was there a sudden leap in numbers coming directly from China.

Emigration from Asian, African, Middle Eastern and Latin American societies to Australia has naturally increased substantially since 1975. These societies make up the great majority of the world's population and most of their inhabitants were previously excluded from Australia. However, those coming to Australia are in no sense typical of those they leave behind, nor do all countries contribute in equal proportion to their populations. Indian migration to Australia is much less than to Canada and the United States. Bangladesh and Pakistani migration is negligible when contrasted with the very large numbers who have gone to Britain or the Middle East. Filipino and Korean migration to North America is much greater than to Australia, despite recently increasing numbers. Most African migration comes from European populations in Southern Africa and most Latin American migration is from the predominantly European societies of Chile, Argentina and Uruguay.

Much of the debate about Asian migration in recent years seems to have been sparked by concerns about the major Indo-Chinese and Lebanese populations, who have mainly been motivated by a desire to escape from intolerable local conditions. These communities have high rates of unemployment, low levels of English proficiency and high levels of concentration in metropolitan areas of Sydney. Opinion polling in the late 1980s has found them to be the least popular major groups in Australian society, along with Muslims in general. These attitudes correspond to those in other societies, where the poor and disadvantaged are not regarded favourably by the majority, especially if they are of a markedly different ethnic character. Yet the impact of overt racism in Australia appears to be slight and not to threaten domestic stability. Nothing comparable to the race riots of the United States and Britain, or the rise of racist parties in France, has been encountered in Australia. While some critics of the immigration and multicultural programs have predicted such developments, they have yet to materialise. Most non-Europeans in Australia have integrated into society just as smoothly and quickly as their European predecessors. As suggested above, many were already familiar with British-derived institutions and practices before arrival and many are well placed in the middle classes. Race, in the sense of physical appearance, has proved less important than refugee status, lack of language skills and lack of economic and educational resources. In many respects Australia now shares the experience of Canada and the United States in creating a substantial business and professional class of Asian origin.

CHAPTER EIGHT

CREATING MULTICULTURAL AUSTRALIA

*A*ustralia in 1947 was one of the most monocultural societies in the world. Today, it is often wrongly claimed to be one of the most multicultural. Accepting that Australia did have cultural variety in 1947 and is still predominantly oriented to the English-speaking world, what processes have produced change and how important are they?

In 1947 the proportion of Australians born overseas, at less than 10%, was the lowest since records were first kept in 1828. Of those born elsewhere, 6% were from the British Isles and only 3% from the rest of the world. The Aboriginal population was only 87 000, having risen from a low point of 74 000 in 1933. The Asian-born or -descended population was even less. Australia could claim to be 99% white and 96% British, though public statements often put the latter percentage higher.

The major cultural differentiation was between Catholics and Protestants, reflecting Irish and British origins in most cases. Catholics numbered only 19% and were declining. Anglicans were the largest single denomination, suggesting that Australians of English origin were the largest element of the population. The 1947 Census does not record language use, but it seems probable that at least 98% spoke only English. In the Census of 1986 Australia appeared to be far more varied than it was forty years before, though many rural and provincial areas had scarcely changed. Provincial New South Wales, rural Tasmania and large areas of Queensland are no more multicultural today than they were in 1947. Quite important cities such as Ballarat, Bendigo, Launceston,

Toowoomba or even Newcastle, are not significantly different. The proportion of Aborigines in the Northern Territory population is lower than it was in 1947, although still by far the highest in Australia. The impact of post-war immigration on Australia has been uneven and national figures disguise considerable variety.

Despite this, the contrasts are very obvious. Twenty-two per cent of Australians were born overseas, or more than twice the 1947 proportion in a population which is more than twice as big. Fourteen per cent normally use a language other than English, or seven times the 1947 level. Catholics are now the largest religious denomination in nominal terms and by far the largest in practising terms. Those of non-European descent, including Aborigines, now make up 5% of the total or at least five times the 1947 level at the height of White Australia. Four times the proportion of 1947 have been born in countries other than the United Kingdom and Ireland. Perhaps most importantly there are now large populations derived from countries which, in 1947, had virtually no presence in Australia, such as Vietnam, the Philippines, Chile, Turkey, Sir Lanka, the Netherlands and Egypt.

This multicultural variety is most visible in the major cities of Sydney, Melbourne, Adelaide, Perth, Brisbane, Wollongong, Geelong, Canberra and Darwin. It is present but less significant in Newcastle, the Gold Coast and Hobart. In rural and mining areas the multicultural presence is largely confined to the Pilbara, Mount Isa, the Murrumbidgee and Murray irrigation areas and north Queensland, areas which were already recruiting foreign workers before 1947. Australian multiculturalism today is an urban phenomenon, compared with nineteenth century ethnic variety both in Australia, in the United States and in Canada. There is little likelihood of distinctive ethnic societies like the Barossa Germans maintaining their social boundaries for as long as was possible a century ago. Yet the changes in the major cities are fundamental, as is the rapidly changing concept of nationhood in a society which is no longer tied to its British origins in anything but sentiment or language.

It was not the intention of the post-war planners that such variety would be created. Apart from their dedication to the idea of a White Australia, they were essentially assimilationists. While many in the Chifley government were second generation

Irish Catholics, they were also Australian nationalists. The government introduced Australian citizenship for the first time and Chifley became the first Australian citizen on Australia Day 1949. There were two conflicting expectations of immigrants. One was that they would become real Australians, while the conservative side of politics was still happy to talk about them as becoming British. This dichotomy had lasted for a century. The new Australian flag had been attacked as an 'Irish flag' in the early years of the twentieth century because it replaced the British Union Jack. Many were unable to distinguish between the two loyalties, which they saw as completely compatible with each other. In September 1939 Prime Minister Menzies had simply proclaimed that as Britain was at war, Australia was also at war. The welcoming of American troops to defend Australia in 1942 was criticised by the Opposition as implying disloyalty to Britain, despite the defeat of Britain in Singapore. British citizens enjoyed all the benefits of Australian citizenship except that they could be excluded from entry or deported, powers rarely and controversially used against white British from the United Kingdom. It was not until 1984 that the automatic right to vote was withdrawn from British citizens arriving in Australia. Those coming before that date still retain that right, whether naturalised Australians or not.

All previous immigration policy had been designed to maintain the British character of Australia. This objective was restated by Calwell when launching the Displaced Persons program in 1947. Non-British immigrants were to be called 'New Australians', a term previously used for British arrivals in the 1920s. The implication was that they were on the way to becoming Australians and would be fully assimilated within their lifetime and preferably as quickly as possible. Assimilationism had been official policy at least since the 1880s, one of the objections to non-Europeans being that because of their appearance they could never truly assimilate. Assimilationism meant the abandoning of all characteristics that made individuals visible in a crowd. This included the public use of languages other than English, the wearing of unusual clothing, gestures not normally used, physical appearance and anything which prevented the individual from becoming invisible to the majority. These expectations were clearly spelled out in official welcoming material. Similar expectations had previously been imposed on German Jewish refugees in 1938 by those from the Australian Jewish community responsible for their settlement.

Not surprisingly, few could reach these high standards. Many British immigrants had strong regional accents, though they were not as readily identifiable by their clothing as many from industrial districts had been in the 1920s. But Europeans could not conform on any dimension. If they could not speak English they were expected to remain silent in public. If they attempted to communicate in a strong accent they were frequently ridiculed. If they wore the clothes they brought from German camps or carried brief cases, they were immediately identifiable as 'reffos'. There were no laws requiring conformity. But Australian society had strongly developed and often rigid notions of what was acceptable and what was not. The task of the government was to develop policies and attitudes which would not disturb those notions, while at the same time extending to 'New Australians' a sufficient welcome to prevent their total alienation from the society which they were being urged to join. But there was continued emphasis on the British character of Australia, which became more open after Menzies' return to power in 1951.

All immigration, settlement and citizenship policy until the 1970s was designed to maintain British privileges. The greatest beneficiaries were, of course, those from the United Kingdom. However some other British subjects, especially the Maltese, were also able to benefit. Throughout Australia's history, New Zealanders have been treated as though they were internal rather than international migrants, a policy still substantially in place. Non-British immigrants were expected to abandon their alien ways and become Australian. No such demands were made upon British and New Zealanders.

The successful settlement of immigrants requires that they learn the language of the host society, comply with and understand its laws, pay its taxes and abandon or modify practices which are illegal or socially unacceptable. It is also highly desirable that immigrants should find suitable work and housing and be able to form a family should they wish to. Australian governments have taken a responsibility for most of these requirements, often building on practices already established a century or more ago such as the provision of basic information on employment and costs. But the first contingent of European immigrants after 1947 was exceptional. They were Displaced Persons and thus destitute. This put an even greater obligation upon government than before, but it also put government in the position of being able to demand conformity. Short of coercion, quite unacceptable in a democracy, there was no way that adult Europeans, many of them refugees because they were nationalists, could be made to abandon their languages and culture simply because Australian public opinion demanded that they should. Official policy was thus largely exhortatory. It attempted to explain to the public that foreign migrants were an asset and to the migrants that they were lucky to be in Australia and should conform to its norms.

The housing and employment needs of the refugees were met through placement in camps and compulsory direction to jobs. This kept the migrants away from the cities for two years and often left them to socialise only with other migrants, though not necessarily those from the same country. From 1951 onwards the drift to the major cities became marked and significant numbers of Europeans began to settle in industrial areas of Melbourne, Adelaide, Newcastle and Wollongong. They did not form distinct residential enclaves, as many assimilationists had feared. There are no visibly Polish, Ukrainian or Baltic areas in Australian cities. But they did form an elaborate network of social, cultural and educational clubs, all designed to preserve language and ethnic variety and to pass it on to their children. Most of the eastern European communities in Australia are still highly organised around such activities.

The first stage in establishing multicultural Australia was also the most difficult. The formation of distinct ethnic organisations, dedicated to the maintenance of foreign languages and culture, was not welcomed by public opinion nor by officials. The Good Neighbour movement conducted most of its affairs only in English and many of its activists were assimilationists who resisted attempts by immigrants from Europe to gain influence and positions. Many migrants were content with a passive role or with the affairs of their communities. Some were very anxious to conform and to assimilate as quickly as possible. Those who were culturally and linguistically close to the British, such as the Dutch and the Germans, had less trouble in conforming than the Ukrainians or Croatians. Official policy was to assist Dutch, German and Scandinavian immigrants, who were assumed to be more assimilable than those from eastern or southern Europe.

However, from the mid-1950s onwards it became increasingly hard to attract migrants from societies which were now stabilised and prosperous again. It was also much harder to keep out those from the poorer societies of southern Europe which had already sent thousands of immigrants in the 1920s, creating links which were reactivated in the 1950s.

As numbers from Italy, Greece, Malta and Yugoslavia grew, it became obvious that the dream of rapid assimilation would not be realised. While the Good Neighbour movement had good contacts with British migrants and Displaced Persons, it never made much progress with southern Europeans. The final abandoning of the movement in 1978 was a belated recognition that it was not possible to settle immigrants by methods which had been developed for British immigrants in the 1920s and for later refugees. Southern Europeans were not refugees, were strongly motivated towards economic success but were also poorly educated and monolingual. The great majority became factory workers with little spare time for re-education. They were able to build on small communities established before the Second World War and to develop new clubs and media to cater for greatly increased numbers. Because they were so numerous, they could recreate the life they had left behind to a greater degree than many eastern European refugees. They were not as consciously committed to maintaining language and culture as were many of the more politically motivated DPs. But the Greeks in particular had a long experience of preserving the Greek language and religion in the hostile environment of the Ottoman empire as well as in Greek colonies scattered around the Mediterranean and the Black Sea. The Maltese, who had been brought up and educated within a British colony, appeared to be the most likely to assimilate. But they were also highly concentrated in the western suburbs of Melbourne and Sydney and many of their social contacts were therefore with other Maltese in the same areas.

While the eastern Europeans had consciously resisted assimilation, the southern Europeans simply ignored it. Their social life took place mainly in an ethnic setting. Many of them worked with compatriots in large factories where it was management policy to place workers from the same background together to facilitate communication. The numbers settling in major cities were so large that businesses grew up to cater for compatriots, in contrast to the pre-war businesses which mainly served the Anglo-Australian majority. Not all southern Europeans were manual workers and a class of professionals developed which also catered mainly for their fellow countrymen. It was possible to engage in most normal activities without recourse to the English language or without much interaction with the majority. Exhortations about living in ghettoes or not being active in the community were simply irrelevant to people who had a very highly developed community and family life of their own.

The first official recognition that rapid assimilation was impracticable came as early as 1964 when the Assimilation branch of the Department of Immigration was renamed the Integration branch. This was partly in response to criticism at the annual Citizenship Conventions which had been held since 1950. But the most open repudiation of assimilationism, like the ending of racial discrimination in selection, followed the election of the Whitlam government in 1972. This declared, through the minister for immigration, Al Grassby, that Australia was a multicultural society, a term taken from Canada where it had been in use since about 1968. Despite attempts to define multiculturalism by advisers to government such as Professor George Zubrzycki, the term remained rather vague until the 1978 report of the committee on migrant programs and services, chaired by Frank Galbally.[1]

Official support for multiculturalism at the Commonwealth level has been unbroken since the early 1970s. Three prime ministers, Gough Whitlam, Malcolm Fraser and Bob Hawke, reasserted their support for the concept of multiculturalism and for institutions to give it effect.

Multiculturalism as official policy has gone through a number of phases, corresponding to partisan reinterpretation and politicians' assessment of public opinion. In the early 1970s there was no national organisation claiming to speak for non-British immigrants. State ethnic communities' councils began to be formed in 1975, owing much to the initiative of Bill Jegorow of Sydney. The New South Wales council has remained the strongest ever since. In 1979 councils existed in all states and territories and they were organised into the Federation of Ethnic Communities' Councils of Australia, with its headquarters in Sydney. By the 1980s there was a national voice from the ethnic constituency, which scarcely existed a decade before. FECCA has received financial support from the Commonwealth as a representative and consultative body with a wide variety of affiliates. It has consistently supported multiculturalism in its publications, at its conferences and in direct representations to government. No other body can claim to speak for ethnic minorities in this way. Its support for multiculturalism has been essential in sustaining government commitment.

There are, however, other avenues through which policy has been developed. Prominent individuals with access to politicians, and particularly to prime ministers, have worked outside the FECCA structure by direct lobbying. Major communities such as the Jews (who have been centrally organised as a lobby since 1944), the Italians (who have no single national organisation) or the Greeks (who have been particularly influential), prefer to operate within the party political arena and by personal contact, rather than through the formal structures of FECCA. But apart from the Greeks, few non-British ethnic minorities have been well represented in elected parliaments.

Multiculturalism has been accepted as public policy nationally and in most states because politicians have perceived a demand for it from immigrant communities, which have been increasing their electoral strength. This is a legitimate part of the democratic process, previously developed by Catholics in defence of their interests. Aborigines have also become much more politically influential since the early 1970s. But in Australian history ethnic input into public policy making was unusual, because ethnic minorities were unusual. In contrast to Canada, the United States and the United Kingdom, ethnic minorities have not sent many representatives directly into parliamentary politics, nor have they formulated coherent demands on the public purse or the legislative process. This is partly because most ethnic communities in Australia are still in the immigrant phase, where political effectiveness is inhibited by language difficulties or by lingering interest in homeland politics irrelevant to Australia. In other societies, and for Irish Australians in the past, the second generation is often more influential than the first. Yet it would be wrong to suppose that multicultural policies were simply adopted to placate an 'immigrant vote'. Such policies have been very popular with that part of the Australian people who derive from somewhere other than the British Isles. Governments of both major parties have subscribed to them since the mid-1970s despite some criticism among conservatives in the mid 1980s.

The historic development of Australian multiculturalism is best traced through the creation, expansion and alteration of institutions designed to support such policies. There has been no legislative basis to multiculturalism, but there has been a plethora of short-term programs, especially in the field of education. Only since the establishment of the Office of Multicultural Affairs in the Department of Prime Minister and Cabinet in 1987 has the responsibility for public policy moved away from the Department of Immigration, in accordance with the view that 'multiculturalism is for all Ausralians'. The most detailed account of official thinking is contained in the *National Agenda for a Multicultural Australia*, launched by prime minister Bob Hawke in Sydney in 1989.[2]

Between 1973 and 1978 policy was mainly concerned with repudiating assimilationism and with preventing racial or ethnic discrimination. In turning their backs on almost a century of discriminatory and assimilationist history, politicians might have taken a serious risk, had not both Whitlam and Fraser agreed that such a history had to be rejected in the interests of national harmony. The legislative and institutional changes included the *Racial Discrimination Act* of 1975 and the establishment of a Commissioner for Community Relations. Both the law and the commissioner had universal objectives, in not being confined to immigrant issues. Aborigines were seen as likely targets of discrimination and became the most important ethnic group using the available protection.

The Fraser government became aware of growing organisation amongst immigrant groups through the long association of some eastern Europeans with the Liberal Party, the establishment of ethnic communities' councils and the increasing strength of southern Europeans in many electorates and their apparent tendency to support Labor. Fraser's most important initiative was to implement the Galbally recommendations of 1978. These called for greater recognition in government services that many clients could not speak English; for immigrant welfare to be delivered through subsidised ethnic organisations; for official support for community languages and media; and for the setting up of a research institute which would refine the concept of multiculturalism and develop knowledge about Australian cultural variety. These recommendations created a network of ethnic welfare workers and migrant resource centres, which still exists. They encouraged the development of ethnic radio and multicultural television through the Special Broadcasting Service (SBS). An Institute of Multicultural Affairs was set up in Melbourne in 1979, although it was abolished by the Hawke government in 1986. With this exception, most of the Galbally proposals are still in place. Between 1978 and 1983 ethnic affairs commissions were set up in the Labor governed states to develop similar policies at the state level. In 1980 SBS 0/28 began television broadcasts in Sydney and Melbourne in a variety of languages.

Between 1973 and 1980, public policy became firmly committed to multiculturalism and official funds were expended on a variety of institutions and programs. There was little public opposition to these developments and growing enthusiasm for them in the ethnic communities, whose leaders took an increasing role in advising government and pressing for changes in education, welfare and public administration. The return of Labor nationally in 1983 did not disturb most existing practices but strengthened the idea that multiculturalism was concerned with social justice and equity rather than simply with the maintenance of minority languages and cultures. Cuts to multicultural and educational programs in 1986, including the abolition of the Institute and a proposal to merge SBS with the Australian Broadcasting Commission, were strongly resented by the ethnic communities. The government reversed some of the changes and publicly identified itself with multiculturalism once again. It created the Office of Multicultural Affairs and transferred functions which had previously rested with the Department of Immigration, signalling that it gave a higher priority to the policy than in the past.

By following Canada in officially declaring Australia to be multicultural, successive governments have not only departed from past history but have also been more innovative than some other immigrant societies, including the United States. With exceptions in Sweden and the Netherlands, European States have been very reluctant to acknowledge the changes which substantial immigration is making. Germany does not recognise the concept of multiculturalism at all and France still adheres to a long assimilationist tradition. Britain, like the United States, recognises the reality in its educational and media systems, but does not proclaim cultural variety as a national objective. Israel, which shares with Australia the distinction of having more overseas-born citizens than any other developed country, officially aims at a Jewish State with many origins but a broadly common culture, religion and language. Thus it is worth asking why Australia has made such a strong public commitment and what it means by that commitment in long-term historical terms rather than in the pragmatic programs of the short-term. An important factor is the very large and historically sudden changes to the character of the Australian people in the past forty years. This made it probable, on the experiences of other societies and pre-war Australia, that there would be social tensions between those of differing ethnicity. One argument for multiculturalism is simply that it gives official blessing to harmonious community relations, in the same way as public exhortations in the 1950s gave a similar blessing to assimilation. A second argument is that as rapid assimilation failed for many immigrants, nothing is to be gained from its continued espousal, especially as such immigrants become citizens and participants in the democratic process. Demands that immigrants become 'real Australians' were seen by the late 1960s as a reason for increasing return rates to Europe, although economic improvement at home was probably more important. There was little sense in encouraging large numbers to come to a society in which they would feel unwanted.

Multiculturalism also developed as a pragmatic response to the problems of extending government services to taxpayers who could not effectively use them because they were delivered only in English on the assumption of ethnic homogeneity. This was an important aspect of the Galbally recommendations and was given even more prominence in the Hawke government's 'access and equity' strategy after 1986, developed by the Office of Multicultural Affairs. This tried to ensure that all government agencies built into their aims the servicing of those of non-English-speaking background.[3] A similar approach has been adopted in most states, following the pioneering programs in New South Wales from 1978. Multiculturalism as an aspect of social justice was also concerned with the opportunities open to immigrants and their children through the education system and the labour market. This included a range of programs, including education for those whose mother tongue was not English, recognition of overseas qualifications and equal employment opportunity on lines previously adopted for women in Australia and elsewhere.

As the composition of immigration changed from the mid-1970s, policy once again became concerned with racial intolerance and good community relations. The rise of small but virulent racist groups, and the public discussion about Asian immigration between 1984 and 1988, gave force to the idea that multiculturalism was concerned with social harmony, a concept developed in the late 1960s. As in the 1950s, though rather more hesitantly, government advised the public that no threat was presented by the admission of large numbers of a different culture. Opinion polling in the late 1980s suggests that about half the population agreed while half did not. Assimilationist attitudes were much stronger than overt racism. Strongest feelings were towards Muslims, Arabs and Vietnamese, while previously rejected groups such as Chinese, Jews or Aborigines were viewed more tolerantly than in the past. The inheritance of White Australia was undoubtedly still present. But it did not manifest itself in organised or political racism, despite the debates of the 1980s.

The aspect of multiculturalism which was most important to ethnic and immigrant groups, but which aroused most public hostility, was cultural and linguistic maintenance. This was often supported by conservative ethnic leaders but just as fervently opposed by conservatives from the majority Anglo-Australian population. In contrast to Canada, Australia has placed little emphasis on the preservation of immigrant cultures. The Special Broadcasting Service represents the most expensive single commitment by government towards this end. But it is doubtful whether it is very influential, as its television services are watched by relatively small numbers. Video cassettes in various languages are probably as important for language maintenance, although little is known about their use and impact. Government has also committed itself since the Galbally report to subsidising weekend ethnic schools and the teaching of community languages in normal day schools. The national language policy, adopted in 1988, is the major instrument for sustaining these approaches. Some ethnic groups, such as Greeks, Croatians and Ukrainians, have been very successful in passing on their languages and traditions to locally-born descendants, while others, such as Dutch and Germans, have not. Factors within the ethnic community, such as the centrality of language to ethnic self-definition, are probably more important in these processes than is official encouragement or subsidy. Subsidy is important in support for religious schools, where Jewish, Greek Orthodox and Islamic schools now share in the funds previously available only to Catholics and Protestants.

Multiculturalism has developed from an immigrant settlement program, with pragmatic objectives, into an ideology which redefines Australians as drawn from many sources rather than simply from the British Isles. It allows scope for Aborigines to be drawn into multicultural programs, though for political and administrative reasons Aborigines have developed their concept of nationality and their demands on government separately. Despite conservative criticism, it does not endorse complete cultural relativity. From its origins in the early 1970s it has been a liberal democratic belief, which holds that all Australians should accept certain core values and forms of behaviour. In the absence of any serious ethnic conflict between immigrant and native Australians, the charge that multiculturalism 'does not work' must be questioned. Government has taken a central role in gaining public acceptance for mass immigration ever since the late 1940s. It has changed its basic ideology from assimilation to multiculturalism, partly as a response to reality, partly as a response to the views of immigrants, and partly as evidence of increasing tolerance of variety in society as a whole. Naturally many Australians are still strongly influenced by the traditions of the past, which were not multicultural and which were based on fear of difference. But such traditions are counter-productive for the well-being of such a varied people as the Australians of today.

CHAPTER NINE

DEBATING IMMIGRATION AFTER TWO HUNDRED YEARS

*F*or 200 years Australia has been building its population through immigration. In this process the Aboriginal inhabitants were displaced over most of the continent and reduced to a small minority, although one which is increasing in numbers. A majority of Australians are descended from British and Irish immigrants from the years before 1930. But at least 40% are either immigrants themselves or the children of immigrants. One-in-five are not significantly of British or Irish descent and about one-in-twenty are not of European descent. For most of the past two centuries it has been assumed that an Australian people would be created through continuing immigration. Migration was to be controlled to produce long-term social consequences. Between 1788 and the 1940s the object was to reproduce a British people who would be drawn from the different peoples and religions of the British Isles but not, significantly, from elsewhere. Between the 1880s and the 1970s this aim was refined to exclude anyone not of European descent and appearance. In times of expansion skills have been ignored in favour of numbers. In more recent years the reproduction of a skilled and educated people has been sought much more actively than before the 1940s. At all times it has been assumed that there was plenty of room for new arrivals, who were expected to maximise the national and their own wealth by hard work.

Mass immigration was only suspended when it was felt that there were not enough jobs for those who had already arrived or that excess numbers had to be absorbed before newcomers could be added. This was true for the 1890s, the 1930s and the early 1970s. Some areas of Australia have consistently sought new immigrants. Others, such as South Australia or Queensland, have only done so at particular times of rapid expansion. Tasmania has seldom attracted large numbers and has tended to lose its native-born to the mainland, a process already causing concern over a century ago. Attempts to people 'the empty north' have not been very successful away from the Queensland coast. As recently as 1989 the Northern Territory and its main city, Darwin, both recorded population losses. Outback areas of Queensland and New South Wales have been losing people for generations and are the areas least likely to attract new settlers. Most immigrants do not settle on the land nor is there much freely available land on which to settle, in contrast to the mid-nineteenth century. This simply reproduces in Australia the common experience of all other developing countries. Modern civilisations are urban and those moving to them seek an urban location.

Most public debate about immigration in the past centred around the ethnic character of immigrants or their suitability as settlers. The ending of convict recruitment provoked the first of these debates in the 1840s, both in Australia and in Britain. It was felt that transportation was inhuman, but also that it was uneconomic. Free settlers, as in South Australia, would have an incentive to work, breed and prosper which convicts lacked. They would add to the value of their property rather than being a drain on the public purse. They would be drawn from the productive classes of overpopulated England, Scotland and Ireland and should be subsidised to come to Australia rather than coerced as with the convicts, or lost to America as with so many Irish. Opposition to transportation and support for assisted free settlement meshed well with liberal notions of the free movement of goods, capital and labour. These ideas dominated debates about immigration for a century. They were modified by British and Australian desires to keep the colonies British by not encouraging too many foreigners to settle and thus risk the loss of allegiance which had led to the defection of the United States from the British empire.

The components of public debate in the middle years of the nineteenth century included a number of beliefs: that the Aboriginal population could not form the basis of an agricultural workforce and should be displaced or confined to industries such as cattle droving for which they seemed suited;

that the British character of Australia must be preserved in the interests of Britain and that the Australian economy should be tied in all respects to that of Britain; that British forms of agriculture and industry should be reproduced in Australia and this was best done through importing British workers; that British political and social institutions should be recreated in Australia by and for a British people; that it was in the interests of Britain to allow its labour surplus to move freely within the empire which would thus grow more prosperous to the advantage of Britain; that only those who could work effectively, create and raise families and not become a charge on the public purse should be subsidised to immigrate; that Britain, as the strongest power in the world, would protect the interests of its colonists, who were expected to remain loyal to the land of their origin.

There were areas of dispute even within this broad consensus about the national purposes. Loyalty to both England and Ireland became increasingly difficult as the interests of these two components of the United Kingdom came into conflict at home. Those that Britain sought to send away were not always those that Australia wished to attract. The interests and attitudes of the native-born (who were a minority until the 1880s) were not always those of the imperial power. Local labour did not always welcome new arrivals who were poorer and more willing to undercut high local wages. The hierarchical and conservative aspects of British institutions did not sit easily with the liberal and even radical attitudes of many immigrants. The position of non-British aliens remained anomalous as they were free to arrive and settle but not always to own land or to be full citizens.

The focus of the debates shifted in the second half of the century towards the maintenance of racial purity. From simply assuming that the British were superior to all others, public opinion moved towards grading people of different appearance and culture in terms of their superiority and inferiority to each other. The notion of a 'tree of life' was widespread, with Australian Aborigines on the lowest branches and northern Europeans on the highest. Such ideas were widespread until the 1940s, with their greatest international impact resulting from the rise of the German Nazi party between 1933 and 1945. In Australia racist ideas were consensual between the 1880s and the 1940s. White Australia was described as a 'settled policy' and thus not open to debate or critical comment. Indeed, there was no debate on this area of immigration policy for the first half of the twentieth century except at the fringes of politics in such organisations as the Communist Party. The major debate was over the extent to which Australia could absorb the surplus millions of Britain in what was often described as an empty land. The Australian national anthem still promises that 'for those who've come across the seas, we've boundless plains to share'. Only the onset of the depression of the 1930s brought this optimism into question.

Basic ideas of Australia as empty, welcoming to the British and confined to whites were still consensual when the postwar program began in 1947. The debate was largely over numbers and the capacity to absorb. Unionists felt that mass migration might threaten wages and conditions, as some had argued since the early 1840s. The achievement of Calwell and Chifley was to argue that nothing in the labour or housing market would be disturbed because non-British arrivals would be put into camps and directed to work which Australians would not undertake. Apart from these pragmatic arguments, the program was also described as idealistic. One ideal was the strengthening of White Australia to the point where it could no longer be threatened from Asia. Another was the rescuing of thousands of Europeans from wartime devastation and from communism. A third was the welcoming of disadvantaged refugees by a generous and charitable people who were ready to share their wealth and freedom. The debate about post-war migration was very muted, as all interested parties were co-opted into support for the program and both sides of politics agreed on its desirability. Such discordant voices as were raised were either from the labour movement, worried about competition for jobs, or from Protestants, worried about the Catholic preponderance amongst refugees. There were also some who felt that the politics of the DPs were unacceptable in Australia, and this argument was strengthened when Germans were given assisted passages in 1952.

Public debate in the 1940s and 1950s was muted by several factors. There was growing prosperity based on full employment, much of it created by immigrant labour. There were no social disorders which could be traced to alien migration. Australia was still regarded as thinly populated and under Asian threat (though from China and Indonesia rather than

Japan). The presence of noticeable numbers in the streets who were visibly non-British was confined to Melbourne, Sydney, Adelaide and Wollongong and then only to some areas of those cities. All public life remained British-Australian in character and there was a revival of Australian nationalism directed against Britain rather than against 'New Australians'. The political parties did not want immigration to become an issue and it was never raised in election campaigns by any of them. If there were 'problems' caused by immigration, they were those of the migrants and did not impinge on the great majority of Australians.

There was, then, little in the way of public debate about immigration until the 1960s. However, some issues were starting to be raised at the margins of established public life. The Communist Party, which was at its most influential between 1942 and 1956, opposed the White Australia Policy. It made early attempts to create links with Yugoslav, Italian and Greek migrants though it could hardly do so with eastern European refugees from communism. The Catholic Social Movement (later the National Civic Council) was also opposed to White Australia and was able to link up with the anti-communists among the New Australians. Opposition to White Australia also grew among Protestant intellectuals, particularly at Melbourne University. The Immigration Reform Group was founded in 1959 and had some influence on the debate in the Australian Labor Party although firmly resisted by its then leader, Arthur Calwell. All these movements were on the margin of conventional politics but they had some influence on different publics. The admission of Asian students into Australian universities under the Colombo Plan was an important factor in making Australian students favourable to relaxation. However, the movement was largely confined to the University of Melbourne, where it campaigned in the 1961 federal elections.

A second marginal influence on public debate was starting to emerge from the 'ethnic communities' which had been formed by immigrants, and through the ethnic media which catered for those unable to speak English. All ethnic minorities tend to form organisations for self-help and social purposes: Jewish organisations have existed in Australia since 1817; the first German-language paper was published in South Australia in 1848; some Chinese clubs can trace their origins back to the 1850s; and the oldest mosque still functioning in Australia was founded in Perth in 1904. What happened after 1947 was thus not new but it was different in scale. The sudden arrival of large numbers of Italians, Greeks and Yugoslavs in the 1950s created whole networks of clubs and media in the major cities. The determination of Eastern European refugees to maintain their languages and their political positions had already had the same effect from the late 1940s. Official policy did not recognise this development, preferring to reach migrants through mainstream charitable groups organised by the Good Neighbour Councils. Wartime restrictions on the foreign language press remained until 1956, ensuring that articles were accompanied by an English translation. But ethnic organisations were not illegal and could not be suppressed or ignored in a liberal democracy.

The growth of an 'ethnic lobby' was slow but becoming noticeable by the late 1960s. As many aliens were not yet naturalised or could not effectively speak English, their political impact was relatively slight. However, the split in the Labor Party after 1955, and the continuing salience of communism as a domestic issue throughout that decade, gave eastern Europeans a higher profile than they might otherwise have had. Parallel attempts by the Communists to appeal to Italians and Greeks were also noticed with alarm by some public figures. The established political parties were reluctant to accept this development though the New South Wales Liberals set up a New Australian Committee in 1954. Trade union-dominated Labor Parties were very suspicious of eastern Europeans because of their conservatism and of southern Europeans because of the legacy of hostility from pre-war years. But some Labor politicians, most notably Gough Whitlam, Al Grassby and Don Dunstan, were very conscious of the changes taking place in some Labor electorates and in the working class in general. It was assumed by many politicians and commentators well into the 1960s that immigrants were more conservative than native Australians. Consequently Labor tended to be hostile towards them while the Liberals took them for granted.

The major demands emerging from the largely hidden ethnic constituency were for an end to assimilation and for a recognition that non-English-speaking immigrants needed special educational and welfare services. The issue of White

Australia was not generally canvassed at this stage by ethnic organisations, which were mainly European in makeup. Official thinking started moving away from crude assimilationism by the mid-1960s. There was growing discontent with the paternalism which many perceived in the attitudes of the religious and charitable bodies making up the Good Neighbour Councils. Cultural and language maintenance, which had always been high priorities for the DP generation, were also important to Greeks and Italians, who had become much more numerous.

The growing opposition to assimilationism was taken up by the newly elected Labor government of Gough Whitlam, which pronounced itself committed to multiculturalism in 1973. The Whitlam government also announced that immigration would no longer be based on race, colour or national origin, thus ending the White Australia Policy. There was surprisingly little partisan opposition to these changes, reflecting the extent to which the new leadership of the Liberal Party had abandoned the settled policies previously espoused by Sir Robert Menzies. Nor was the Labor Party resistant to changes which seemed to go against its basic White Australia principles, set forth in party platforms since its beginnings in the 1890s. The party had already taken this objective out of its platform in 1965, bringing it into line with all major political parties.

It is, perhaps, surprising how easily multiculturalism and universalism were accepted in the public arena in the early 1970s. One explanation is that many other issues were crowding out an overloaded political agenda. The years between 1968 and 1975 were quite turbulent by Australian standards and many social changes were being debated and even implemented.

The partisan consensus on immigration and multiculturalism continued throughout the 1970s. Under Malcolm Fraser, the Liberal Party took an active interest in the immigrant constituency. It endorsed the Galbally report of 1978 very enthusiastically. Its most influential ministers for immigration, Michael Mackellar and Ian Macphee, were on the liberal reformist wing of the party. The ALP, under Whitlam, Hayden and Hawke, came to realise that its voters and its affiliated unionists were drawn to a large extent from immigrant Australians. Outside Queensland, most Labor electorates had a higher than average immigrant population. Labor politicians were consequently approached by immigrant constituents and became very aware of their viewpoints and demands. This process was most marked in Victoria and South Australia. Thus there was no fundamental dispute about multiculturalism or immigration policy except in terms of promising to do better than the other side. Labor continued to have some doubts about anti-communist refugees as in the past. But it was now firmly committed against White Australia and racism, endorsing the approaches institutionalised by Whitlam between 1972 and 1975. While there was little enthusiasm for the new 'ethnic politics' in the National Party or in some sections of the Liberals, the Liberal leader Malcolm Fraser had views on racism and Aborigines which were quite distinct and more radical than those of most of his conservative predecessors.

What then, sparked the continuing debates which have erupted regularly since the early 1980s? One explanation lies in the changed character of public debate both in Australia and in other English-speaking societies, particularly the United States and Britain. The ascendancy of Reagan and Thatcher in the two societies most influential on Australian thinking, encouraged a more militant and critical conservatism to emerge, which is often termed the 'New Right'. In questioning the previous Keynesian consensus in economics and criticising the positive role of the State in social engineering, this school of thought also questioned attempts to eliminate racial discrimination or to alleviate the position of disadvantaged ethnic groups. Some argued, as did Thomas Sowell in the United States, that affirmative action programs for ethnic minorities did no good and might do positive harm. They mainly benefited the middle-class social workers who were paid to administer them. More crudely, many simply saw multicultural or migrant settlement programs as unnecessary expenditures in difficult economic times. Arguments for reducing the functions of the State were also arguments against public programs of any kind. These approaches had their origin amongst conservative economists but influenced reformist parties, including the governing labour parties of Australia and New Zealand.

More conventional conservatives also became vocal during the 1980s as they saw political debate moving in their direction.

Among these the most influential in the Australian context has been Professor Geoffrey Blainey.[1] Blainey's position has developed since his first criticism of increasing Asian immigration in early 1984. Then he was merely saying that public policy was moving ahead of public opinion, which opinion polling suggests is true. However, this has generally been the case for all developments in immigration policy since the 1940s. What has changed in the realm of public opinion is a steadily rising number who are opposed to any immigration at all, which was rarely the case in the expansive 1950s and 1960s. Critics of Blainey have argued that opposition to Asian immigration is only a facet of this general opposition and not its cause.

At no stage has Blainey called for a return to White Australia and neither has anyone influential in public affairs except, perhaps, for some officials of the Returned Services' League. No established interest or viewpoint in Australia now wishes to return to policies which were consensual only thirty years ago. Overt racism is confined to very small and unrepresentative groups, some of whose leaders have been charged with criminal offences. Yet the public debate on the origins of immigrants is undoubtedly influenced by polls showing strong and sometimes majority concern with refugee and Asian intake. Those conservatives who take the populist stance of 'speaking for the people' (of whom Blainey is one) follow in a tradition established by Enoch Powell in regard to immigration to Britain in the 1960s.

Many arguments against a large Asian intake do not take the same form as those used in the past. No-one claims that Asians are inferior or a different order of being. However, many do claim that they are culturally unassimilable or, simply, that the public is not ready for their arrival in large numbers. Arguments against refugee intake are similar to those used against Jews in the 1930s. Refugees are seen as not deserving entry, or as not really being refugees, or as creating problems which should go elsewhere. But they are also seen as coming from alien cultures, such as Vietnam or the Lebanon. Very few admitted as refugees or under the Special Humanitarian Program are of European origin, nor have they been, with some Polish and Soviet exceptions, since 1975. Thus the opposition to refugees overlaps completely the concern about Asian immigration.

In the late 1980s there was growing pessimism about the future of Australian society, based on concern about economic problems. Australia maintained its high living standards. It was not as visibly expansive as in previous decades nor was it much richer than the European societies from which most immigrants had come in the past two centuries. Many of these concerns were focussed by the Bicentennial celebrations of 1988. While Aboriginal issues took centre stage, there was a general feeling that Australia had lost its direction and its national identity. As part of the English-speaking world, Australia was subject to the rapid changes in culture, ideology and outlook which had characterised that world since the 1960s and been conveyed through the mass media. Many of the changes in Australian life were not directly traceable to immigration. But the immigrant presence was so marked by the late 1980s and so different in its sources, that many started to ask whether Australia really needed immigrants at all—a question rarely asked since the 1930s.

In contrast to the Whitlam government, but in common with the Chifley government, the Hawke Labor administration had allowed a steady increase in numbers admitted from the mid-1980s. This policy was endorsed by a major enquiry into immigration policy, headed by Stephen FitzGerald and reporting in 1988 under the title *Immigration: a commitment to Australia.*

The most controversial parts of the report expressed doubts about multiculturalism and urged immigrant acceptance of Australian attitudes and behaviour in terms which were sometimes reminiscent of the 1950s. But the main thrust was that an intake of about 150 000 per annum was desirable on economic grounds and that more emphasis should be placed on the skills and educational levels of immigrants. While no absolute decline in refugee or family reunion programs was recommended, the direction of the report was towards economic rationalism. Immigrants with skills, business experience, higher education or knowledge of a major trading language were to be welcomed. The welfare emphasis in much immigrant settlement policy was to be reduced, in the expectation that such new immigrants would need less assistance than in the past. Immigration, it was argued, would improve the calibre of the workforce and the population in general. This fitted well with public debate about Australia's economic competence to prosper in the competitive world of the Pacific Rim. The sources of immigrants were not seen by FitzGerald as very important. Their economic potential was what counted, not their ethnic or racial origins.

Such an approach was acceptable to the major parties and to economic interests. It was attacked by the ethnic lobby because of its assimilationist rhetoric, much of which the government repudiated. Many of its recommendations were implemented, including the concentration of settlement services on new arrivals, a citizenship drive and a strong emphasis on skills and business acumen in recruiting new immigrants. The main opponents of a continuing high level emerged from the growing conservationist and environmentalist movements, which took an important role in supporting the ALP in the 1990 elections.

While most of the 'Green' movement has been concerned with the Australian environment, a section has taken up the case against population growth, developed by North American writers such as Paul Ehrlich and David Suzuki. In their view the world is not only faced with physical degradation caused by excessive pollution, but also with an almost irreversible population explosion. While the expanding numbers are most visible in the Third World, expanding consumption is most evident in developed countries like Australia. Thus the addition of one Australian to the world's population may do more damage than the birth of fifty Bangladeshis. As at least half of the Australian population increase has come from immigration, it is argued that stabilisation of the Australian population and, preferably, its reduction can only be achieved by ending immigration altogether.[2]

The argument that immigration should be reduced in times of economic difficulties is an old one in Australia, traceable back at least to the depression of the 1840s and being revived in the 1890s, the 1930s and the early 1970s. While most economists (in Australia and overseas) believe that immigration creates jobs rather than taking them from the native-born, such a reaction is understandable. However, in the past it was always assumed that immigration would begin again when times improved. The new argument is that immigration should effectively cease for all time. More moderate advocates of a population policy have supported population stabilisation at 25 million by 2020. This would require a halving of the intake level of the late 1980s to a total of 80 000 admissions, offset against permanent departures.

Whether Australia can stabilise its population by rigorous exclusion of immigrants remains highly doubtful. World population will undoubtedly increase, and States such as China, India and Indonesia will generate a large part of that increase. Pressures for entry into Australia will also increase. Immigration policy is a facet of regional foreign policy, which it has to some extent been ever since Asian States gained their independence in the 1950s. Many of the world's most populous and rapidly increasing societies have touched only lightly upon Australia in the past. Very little immigration has come from Indonesia, Africa, Latin America, Pakistan or Bangladesh. Intake from India and China has been very small in terms of the overall movement from those massive societies. The impact of immigration on Australia has been marked because Australia has such a small population base, not because it is the favoured destination of millions of intending immigrants. This could change rapidly if other immigrant societies, such as the United States and Canada, reduced their intake or if guest worker schemes in Europe or the Middle East were terminated.

If Australia wants to continue its development through migrant intake, as it has done for the past two centuries, it is in an excellent position to do so. If it wants to stabilise its population and remain among the world's least densely populated societies, then it is much less well placed. Domestic pressure to keep a high level of immigration will come from immigrants already in Australia, from industry and commerce and from developmentalists among politicians and academics. These pressures, like all pressures to expand the economy and living standards, will find themselves engaging in the political and intellectual arena with those whose first priority is the protection of the environment against further damage. Debate about immigration cannot remain as muted as it was in the consensual and expansive days of the 1950s and 1960s. Equally, the debate might not be so obsessively concerned with the ethnic and racial origins of newcomers as it has been, at various times, over the past two centuries. Modern Australia was created by mass migration. Its future will depend on resolving further arguments about mass migration.[3]

What the future Australia might look like depends very much on the level and sources of immigration over the next few decades. Already in 1990 the rising numbers of the 1980s went into reverse, mainly due to a drop in New Zealand immigration but also reflecting overseas caution about the Australian economy. The politics of Southeast Asia suggest that large numbers of immigrants will seek to come from Indo-China, the Philippines and Hong Kong. The politics of eastern Europe make it likely that some of the shrinking eastern European communities in Australia will replenish their numbers for the first time since the 1950s, a change that could not have been predicted as recently as the FitzGerald report of 1988. Immigration from Fiji, Polynesia and Sri Lanka seems probable, while events in the Middle East may redirect some of the immigrant guest workers of the Gulf oil States elsewhere.

There is little likelihood that increasing numbers of immigrants will come from Britain or western Europe. The historic connection with Britain is such that it has always provided the largest number of immigrants from a single country. But in the past most such immigrants were encouraged to come by assisted passages, which will not be restored. The unification of Europe and its prosperity and stability will mean that its post-war role in peopling Australia will never return. The most important influences on Australian immigration in the next two decades are likely to be the domestic political and economic situation in Australia, New Zealand and China and the immigration policies of the United States and Canada.

By 2010 about 7% of Australians will be of Southeast or East Asian descent. Chinese, Arabic and Vietnamese will rival Italian and Greek as the most widely used languages after English. Perhaps 2% of the population will be Muslim. Australia will be even more multicultural than it is today. But it will be much less multiracial than the United States or New Zealand. Its population will have passed 20 million but Sydney and Melbourne will still be relatively small cities by world standards. English will still be the language of three-quarters of Australians and two-thirds will still be able to trace their ancestry back to Britain and Ireland. Australia will still be a harmonious multicultural society if it pursues a rational immigration policy consistent with its economic needs and a settlement policy which tries to avoid disadvantage or discrimination. This happy future presupposes economic and social policies which do not create serious disruption or depression. Immigration to Australia will not cause serious problems if it is controlled and planned to utilise the skills and education of new arrivals for the benefit of all.

APPENDICES

Appendix I Chronology

Prior to European settlement, the Australian continent was inhabited by a variety of Aboriginal people, speaking over 200 languages. The length of Aboriginal occupancy is now believed to have been more than 40 000 years, although no definitive date of initial settlement has yet been established. Several different waves may have settled Australia during this long period. The most recent Aboriginal people to settle were the Torres Strait Islanders. There is no undisputed evidence of European contact prior to Dutch discoveries, nor of any permanent non-Aboriginal settlement prior to 1788.

1525   Portuguese established in Timor
1606   First Dutch contact at Cape York peninsula
1642   Tasman claims 'Van Diemen's Land' for the Netherlands
1770   James Cook lands at Botany Bay
1787   British colony of New South Wales established by law
1788   Convict First Fleet lands under Governor Phillip
1791   First convict ship arrives direct from Ireland
1793   First free settlers arrive in New South Wales
1803   Convicts settled in Van Diemen's Land (Tasmania)
1812   Select Committee on Transportation reports to the British Parliament
1824   Convict colony set up in Moreton Bay (Queensland)
1826   Colony of free settlers at Albany, Western Australia
1828   First Census of New South Wales
1829   Free immigrants land at Swan River (Perth)
1831   British regulations allow sale of Crown land to fund assisted passages
1832   Land and Emigration Commission set up in London
1836   First immigrants land in South Australia
1838   Germans settle in South Australia and Queensland
1839   Mainly Scottish settlement at Port Phillip (Melbourne)
1840   Transportation to New South Wales ended
1842   Moreton Bay (Queensland) open for free settlers
1847   First introduction of Pacific Island labourers

1848   Transportation of 'exiles' renewed to Sydney
1849   Caroline Chisholm founds Family Colonization Loan
       Society
1850   First convicts arrive in Western Australia
1851   Discoveries of gold in eastern Australia
1852   Transportation to eastern Australia ended
1853   First Chinese gold-diggers land in Victoria
1855   Victorian legislation to control and limit Chinese
1861   Anti-Chinese riots at Lambing Flat (Young)
1863   Pacific Islanders (Kanakas) brought to Queensland
1868   Last convicts land in Western Australia
1877   Restrictions on Chinese access to Queensland goldfields
1878   Anti-Chinese agitation in Sydney
1880   Intercolonial conference agrees to uniform laws on Chinese
       immigration
1881   First all-Australian Census
1885   Queensland agrees to end Kanaka recruitment
1887   Chinese government enquiry into immigrant conditions
1888   Restrictions on Chinese immigration
1897   Dictation test introduced to control immigrants
1900   *Commonwealth of Australia Constitution Act* gives
       Commonwealth government legal control over immigration
       and citizenship
1901   *Immigration Restriction Act* and *Pacific Island Labourers
       Act* passed by the Commonwealth parliament
1903   *Commonwealth Naturalisation Act* passed
1906   Kanakas repatriated to Pacific Islands
1912   Fairbridge Farm child migration scheme begins
1914   German and Austrian residents interned
1917   German place-names changed in South Australia by law
1920   Commonwealth assumes administrative responsibility for
       immigration
1922   Empire Settlement Act (UK) to encourage assisted
       emigration from Britain
1925   Ferry Commission reports on alien workers in Queensland
1929   Assisted passages terminated
1934   Dictation test applied to Egon Kisch
1936   Jewish refugees start to arrive from Germany
1938   Assisted passages resumed
1939   Enemy aliens interned
1945   Department of Immigration established
1946   Assisted passage agreement with Britain
1947   Start of the Displaced Persons scheme
1948   Australian citizenship created from 1 January 1949
1950   Good Neighbour movement launched nationally
1951   Assisted passage agreements with Netherlands and Italy
1952   Immigration agreements with Germany, Austria and Greece

1955 Arrival of the millionth post-war immigrant
1957 Citizenship after fifteen years available for non-Europeans
1958 *Migration Act* passed, in force from 1 June 1959
1959 Movement against White Australia begins in Melbourne
1964 Assimilation section of Immigration Department becomes the Integration section
1965 Major parties remove White Australia from platforms
1966 Substantial modifications to White Australia Policy
1967 Migration agreement with Turkey
1970 The last migration agreement signed, with Yugoslavia
1971 Bonegilla migrant camp closed after twenty-four years
1973 Official declaration of universal migration policy
1975 *Racial Discrimination Act* passed by Commonwealth
1976 First Vietnamese refugees arrive by boat
1978 Galbally report on migrant programs and services
1979 NUMAS points system introduced for migrant selection
1980 Multicultural television broadcasts start
1981 Assisted passages to end except for refugees
1983 Distinctions between 'British' and 'aliens' ended
1984 Start of the 'Blainey debate' on Asian immigration
1986 Census shows the population as 15.6 million, of whom almost 22% were born overseas
1987 Office of Multicultural Affairs established
1988 FitzGerald report on immigration policy
1989 *National Agenda for a Multicultural Australia* published
1990 Australian population passes 17 million

Appendix II Population of Australia 1788–1986

Year	Aboriginal	Native-born settlers	Overseas-born settlers	Total
1788*	314 500 99.7%	neg. neg.	859 0.3%	315 359 100%
1861*	180 402 13.4%	467 260 34.6%	700 889 52%	1 348 551 100%
1891	110 919 3.4%	2 133 191 65.4%	1 018 164 31.2%	3 262 274 100%
1921	75 604 1.4%	4 596 155 83.4%	839 579 15.2%	5 511 338 100%
1947	87 000 1.1%	6 835 171 89.2%	744 187 9.7%	7 666 358 100%
1961	117 495 1.1%	8 729 406 82.2%	1 778 780 16.7%	10 625 681 100%
1971	150 076 1.2%	10 026 244 78.6%	2 579 318 20.2%	12 755 638 100%
1981	159 897 1.1%	11 382 716 78.1%	3 033 717 20.8%	14 576 330 100%
1986	227 645 1.5%	12 127 130 77.7%	3 247 381 20.8%	15 602 156 100%

Note

- Aboriginal figures are estimates before 1971, based on L. R. Smith: *The Aboriginal Population of Australia*, ANU Press, Canberra, 1980.
- *Figures for 1788 and 1861 are estimates based on data not collected throughout Australia. Total and 'native-born settlers' includes unstated birthplace.
- Percentages are for the total population, including Aborigines. The general source is *Australian Immigration Consolidated Statistics*, AGPS, Canberra (annual) and the colonial and Commonwealth Censuses.

Appendix III Assisted settler arrivals: 1831–1980

Years	Settler arrivals
1831–60	292 595
1861–70	94 674
1871–80	92 930
1881–90	151 818
1891–00	10 918
1901–10	43 731
1911–20	162 185
1921–30	214 851
1931–40	4 609
1941–50	273 195
1951–60	580 758
1961–70	874 610
1971–80	389 849

Source *Australian Immigration Consolidated Statistics*, AGPS, Canberra, annual.

Appendix IV Major birthplaces of the Australian population in 1861, 1901, 1947 and 1986 and as a percentage of total non-Aboriginal population

Birthplace	1861	1901	1947	1986
Australia	467 260 40%	2 908 303 77.2%	6 835 171 90.1%	12 110 456 77.6%
Great Britain	452 311 38.7%	494 689 13.1%	496 454 6.6%	1 057 234 6.8%
Ireland	160 220 13.7%	184 470 4.9%	44 813 0.6%	69 962 0.4%
New Zealand	est 750 0.1%	25 788 0.7%	43 610 0.6%	211 670 1.4%
USA	est 3 750 0.3%	7 448 0.2%	6 232 0.1%	42 383 0.3%
Germany	26 872 2.3%	38 352 1%	14 567 0.2%	114 810 0.7%
Italy	n.a. n.a.	5 678 0.5%	33 632 0.4%	262 435 1.7%
Greece	n.a. n.a.	878 0.1%	12 291 0.2%	137 080 0.9%
China	38 337 3.3%	29 907 0.8%	6 404 0.2%	37 468 0.2%
India	n.a. n.a.	7 637 0.2%	8 160 0.1%	47 820 0.3%

Notes

Figures are for the general area of a country, as boundaries and definitions have changed. Ireland includes both Northern Ireland and the Republic; Great Britain includes the rest of the United Kingdom; Germany includes East and West Germany; Chinese figures had many discrepancies in the colonial censuses and sometimes included Hong Kong.

Appendix V   Overseas-born Australians by birthplace, indicating changes since the effective ending of the White Australia Policy in 1973

Birthplace	1971	1986	Settler arrivals 1986–1990
UK and Ireland	1 088 210	1 127 196	103 334
Southern Europe	669 450	670 002	27 726
Rest of Europe/USSR	452 085	448 247	29 711
North America	42 873	62 819	11 948
Oceania	97 927	264 421	84 108
Latin America	12 879	53 640	17 379
Africa	33 709	77 914	24 682
South Asia	39 960	84 305	25 799
East Asia	28 113	88 293	53 701
Southeast Asia	38 440	240 560	111 810
Middle East	44 352	129 984	30 591
Australian population	**12 755 638**	**15 602 156**	**17 027 00 (est 1990)**

Notes
- Southern Europe includes Italy, Greece, Yugoslavia, Malta, Cyprus.
- North America includes USA and Canada only.
- Oceania is mainly New Zealand.
- Africa includes South Africa but excludes Egypt.
- South Asia includes India and Sri Lanka.
- East Asia includes China, Hong Kong, Japan and Korea.
- Southeast Asia includes Vietnam, Philippines, Malaysia, Indonesia.
- Middle East includes Egypt, Lebanon, Turkey, Iran.

- Definitions vary in different sources but those above are based on Bureau of Immigration Research: *Immigration Update September 1990*, AGPS, Canberra, 1990. Minor adjustments have been made to fit the 1971 figures into this regionalisation.

NOTES

Chapter 1

[1] Convict settlement was not directly relevant to Victoria, which formed part of New South Wales until 1851, but it received many former convicts, especially from Tasmania (Van Diemen's Land).

[2] I. Wyatt (ed.), *Transportees from Gloucestershire to Australia 1783–1842*, Bristol and Gloucestershire Archaeological Society, Gloucester, 1988.

[3] S. Nicholas (ed.), *Convict Workers: Reinterpreting Australia's Past*, Cambridge University Press, Melbourne, 1988.

Chapter 2

[1] *Report of the South Australian House of Assembly Select Committee on Immigration*, Government Printer, Adelaide, 1877.

[2] *Progress Report from the Select Committee on Assisted Immigration*, Government Printer, Sydney, 1880.

[3] A. Martin, *Henry Parkes: a Biography*, Melbourne University Press, 1980.

[4] J. C. Docherty, 'English settlement in Newcastle and the Hunter Valley' in J. Jupp (ed.), *The Australian People*, Angus and Robertson, Sydney, 1988, pp. 406–10.

Chapter 3

[1] John O'Brien, *Around the Boree Log*, Angus and Robertson, Sydney, 1921.

[2] C. Kiernan, *Daniel Mannix and Ireland*, Alella Books, Morwell, 1984.

[3] M. D. Prentis, *The Scots in Australia*, Sydney University Press, 1984.

Chapter 4

[1] The strongest case for Portuguese exploration of Australia is in K. G. McIntyre, *The Secret Discovery of Australia*, Pan Books, Sydney, 1972.

[2] *Report of the Legislative Council Select Committee on Immigration*, Government Printer, Sydney, 1837.

[3] C. F. Yong, *The New Gold Mountain*, Raphael Arts, Adelaide, 1977.

Chapter 5

[1] Based on United Kingdom Board of Trade shipping lists for 1910.

[2] R. G. Appleyard, *The Ten Pound Immigrants*, Boxtree, London, 1988.

[3] J. Jupp, *Arrivals and Departures*, Cheshire-Lansdowne, Melbourne, 1966.

[4] A. Richardson, *British Immigrants and Australia*, Australian National University Press, Canberra, 1974.

[5] Based on an unpublished survey by the United Kingdom Office of Census and Population, London, 1982.

[6] Based on the 1% sample users tape for the 1981 Australian Census.

Chapter 6

[1] E. F. Kunz, *Displaced Persons: Calwell's New Australians*, Pergamon/ANU Press, Sydney, 1988.

[2] *Daily Muiror Souvenir Edition*, 26 October 1950.

[3] *Digest of the Annual Citizenship Convention*, Canberra, 1959.

Chapter 8

[1] F. Galbally (chair), *Migrant Services and Programs*, AGPS, Canberra, 1978.

[2] Office of Multicultural Affairs, *National Agenda for a Multicultural Australia*, AGPS, Canberra, 1989.

[3] J. Jupp (ed.), *The Challenge of Diversity*, AGPS, Canberra, 1989.

Chapter 9

[1] G. Blainey, *All for Australia*, Methuen Haynes, Sydney, 1984.

[2] See e.g. R. Birrell, D. Hill and J. Nevill (eds.), *Populate and Perish?*, Fontana, Sydney, 1984; K. Betts, *Ideology and Immigration*, Melbourne University Press, 1988; and L. H. Day and D. T. Rowland (eds.), *How Many More Australians?*, Longman Cheshire, Melbourne, 1988.

[3] For a summary of current literature see: M. Wooden, R. Holton, G. Hugo and J. Sloan, *Australian Immigration: a survey of the issues*, AGPS, Canberra, 1990.

FURTHER READING

Betts, K. *Ideology and Immigration: Australia 1976 to 1987*. Melbourne University Press, 1988.

Bureau of Immigration Research. *Immigration Update June 1990*. Australian Government Publishing Service, Canberra, 1990.

Charlwood, D. *The Long Farewell: Settlers under Sail*. Allen Lane, Melbourne, 1981.

Collins, J. *Migrant Hands in Distant Lands: Australia's Post-War Immigration*. Pluto Press, Sydney, 1988.

Day, L. H. and Rowland, D. T. *How Many More Australians?* Longman Cheshire, Melbourne, 1988.

Dugan, M. and Szwarc, J. *There Goes the Neighbourhood! Australia's Migrant Experience*. Macmillan and Australian Institute of Multicultural Affairs, Melbourne, 1984.

Hardy, J. (ed.). *Stories of Australian Migration*. New South Wales University Press, 1988.

Hawkins, F. *Critical Years in Immigration: Canada and Australia Compared*. New South Wales University Press, 1989.

Hughes, R. *The Fatal Shore: a History of the Transportation of Convicts to Australia, 1787–1868*. Collins Harvill, London, 1987.

Jupp, J. *Arrivals and Departures*. Cheshire-Lansdowne, Melbourne, 1966.

Jupp, J. (ed.). *The Australian People*. Angus and Robertson, Sydney, 1988.

Kunz, E. F. *Displaced Persons: Calwell's New Australians*. Australian National University Press/Pergamon, 1988.

Lack, J. and Templeton, J. (eds.). *Sources of Australian Immigration History 1901–1945*. History Department, University of Melbourne, 1988.

London, H. I. *Non-White Immigration and the 'White Australia' Policy*. New York University Press, New York, 1970.

Lowenstein, W. and Loh, M. *The Immigrants*. Penguin Books, Melbourne, 1977.

Madgwick, R. B. *Immigration into Eastern Australia 1788–1851*. Sydney University Press, 1969.

Martin, J. I. *The Migrant Presence: Australian Responses 1947–1977*. George Allen and Unwin, Sydney, 1985.

Nicholas, S. (ed.). *Convict Workers: Reinterpreting Australia's Past.* Cambridge University Press, Melbourne, 1988.

O'Farrell, P. *The Irish in Australia*. New South Wales University Press, 1986.

Office of Multicultural Affairs. *National Agenda for a Multicultural Australia*. Australian Government Publishing Service, Canberra, 1989.

Pascoe, R. *Buongiorno Australia: Our Italian Heritage.* Greenhouse Press, Melbourne, 1987.

Prentis, M. D. *The Scottish in Australia*, AE Press, Melbourne, 1987.

Price, C. A. *Southern Europeans in Australia*. Oxford University Press, Melbourne, 1963.

Sherington, G. *Australia's Immigrants 1788–1988*. George Allen and Unwin, Sydney, 1990.

Tampke, J. and Doxford, C. *Australia, Willkommen; a History of the Germans in Australia*. New South Wales University Press, 1990.

Wilton, J. and Bosworth, R. *Old Worlds and New Australia: the Post-War Migrant Experience*. Penguin Books, Melbourne, 1984.

Yarwood, A. T. *Asian Immigration to Australia; the Background to Exclusion 1896–1923*. Melbourne University Press, 1964.

INDEX